STORIES OF STANDARD TEACHING PIECES

CONTAINING EDUCATIONAL NOTES AND LEGENDS PERTAINING TO THE BEST KNOWN AND MOST USEFUL PIANOFORTE COMPOSITIONS IN GENERAL USE BY STUDENTS OF MUSIC AND DESIGNED AS A COMPANION VOLUME TO THE AUTHOR'S "DESCRIPTIVE ANALYSES OF PIANO- FORTE COMPOSITIONS" ❧ ❧ ❧ ❧

BY

EDWARD BAXTER PERRY

THEO. PRESSER CO.,
1712 Chestnut St.,
PHILADELPHIA, PA.

Contents

Stories of Standard Teaching Pieces.

Introduction.

SINCE the publication, some years ago, of my "Descriptive Analyses of Piano Works," and the gratifying reception accorded it by the public, there has been a general and growing demand, especially among teachers, for a volume of similar analyses, dealing with an easier grade of compositions suited to the needs of students.

It is in response to this request that this book has been prepared.

It contains analyses of one hundred pieces available for teaching purposes, while the other volume dealt almost exclusively with the artist's repertoire.

The aim of this work has been the same as in the former volume, viz.: to emphasize the descriptive, emotional, imaginative and suggestive elements in the compositions treated, rather than their mechanical structure or technical details.

It cannot be too often or too forcefully reiterated that good music is a form of ART, a medium of *expression*, appealing to the intelligence, the emotions, and the imagination, not merely to the ear.

It is an important element in education, not a mere pleasant pastime; an ethical and cultural force, not a competitive exhibition of mechanical skill. It is becoming more and more fully recognized as a subtle but powerful factor in the upbuilding of human character, capacity and perceptive faculty; in the development of emotional force, which is the mainspring of action, and of self-control, which is the balance-wheel of the whole life mechanism.

As such, it cannot be ignored and should not be treated merely as a pretty toy, a parlor decoration, or a means of vain display, but should demand our serious attention, our careful study, from its inner and more profoundly significant, not its sensuous and superficial side.

A good composition is a *thought*, a *mood*, or, in some cases, a *scene;* expressed or embodied in a beautiful form; the constituent elements of which are rhythm, melody and harmony. But the form exists merely as the means of expression. Hence any effort to focus the mind of the player or listener upon this inner meaning is legitimate and helpful if rightly understood.

That is the sole purpose and aim of this book. If it serves this purpose the object of the writer will be attained, and his labor repaid.

The compositions herein discussed are, with few exceptions, of a much easier grade, technically, than those in the former volume; hence it is hoped the book will prove of greater practical value to the average teacher and student.

It must be remembered, however, that for that very reason the collection of authentic, historical, legendary and personal data concerning them has been the more difficult.

The great composers naturally put their best efforts and embodied their most important subjects in their larger works; reserving their lighter, less dramatic themes for their smaller compositions, so that from a purely literary standpoint, as reading matter, it has been extremely difficult to maintain the same standard of interest. I can only hope that any deficiencies along this line may be compensated for by the greater pedagogic usefulness of this second volume. It must also be borne in mind that the subject matter is too vast to be entirely covered by any two, or even any twenty such books. I have done what I could and hope still to continue the work.

I have only gathered a few shining pebbles and bright shells scattered on the shore of this great ocean, which I offer for whatever they may be worth. If, by chance, my readers find a few pearls among them, I shall be content.

EDWARD BAXTER PERRY.

Aesthetic Analysis Possible
for Pupils.

Y æsthetic analysis I do not mean musical analysis, that common and necessary branch of instruction more or less efficiently dwelt upon by all the advanced teachers of the age. This latter concerns itself exclusively with the form and workmanship, the architectural structure and details of a composition, which will be good or bad according to the amount of skill, the command of mechanical resources, possessed by the composer. Æsthetic analysis deals with the principles of æsthetics, which are back of all mechanical means and underlie every form of art work. It has to do rather with the essence than with the substance, rather with the matter expressed than with the manner of its expression. It is the analysis of essences or properties; the last crucial test of the musical chemist, reducing a work to its simple elements, in order the more fully to understand and utilize its real value, power and influence in human life.

Æsthetic analysis concerns itself with the spiritual germ, from which every art product is evolved; that conception, evoked from nihility by the creative power of the composer, through a stimulus, which may be either objective or subjective, applied to his imagination and emotions; which conception must always exist prior to any material embodiment, and alone vitalizes such material when embodied.

Let us take for illustration an example of objective stimulus to the artistic activity of a person fittingly constituted and endowed, resulting in an art product, because the sources of subjective stimulus are more difficult to trace and expound.

Suppose some grand and inspiring but not uncommon event, such as a storm at sea, be experienced by a poet, a painter, and a musician, all of whom are endowed with the artistic temperament and talent, and all laborers in the domain of art, though in different departments. Each is stirred to his being's core, and the activity thus engendered seeks to find vent in material expression along the channel familiar to it.

The poet describes to us in words the terror of the tempest-torn deep, the wild winds and weltering waters, the vain struggles of wrecked mariners, and the corpses drifting shoreward in the wan light of a murky dawn. The painter seizes one climactic moment as characteristic of the whole, and gives us in colors, in an expressive tableau, this one single significant situation, from which we must infer what has gone before and what will inevitably follow. His canvas shows us a pall of cloud above a heaving waste of sea, a dismantled ship, just disappearing beneath a sheet of foam, and the tossing arms and blanched faces of her crew in their last brief struggle. The composer, restricted to the medium of tone, gives us all the discordant minor voices of the storm and its impetuous and resistless movement; the shriek of the gale, the roar of answering billows, the mighty sweep of mammoth surges, and the crash of shattering timbers; closing, perhaps, with the remorseful sobbing of the sea, in its subsiding fury, upon a wreck-strewn shore.

Each has treated the theme from a different standpoint, aiming at the same results and effects, but subjecting it to the inherent laws of his own peculiar medium, embodying it in different material, and emphasizing different component elements and their appeal to various faculties and senses. But it is the dread spirit of the storm, which they have caught and imprisoned in every case, and which thrills us with its terrific presence.

Now, while the technical analysis of these different art products would be radically diverse, and in each case is wholly concerned with elements, none of which can be found to figure at all in either of the others, the æsthetic analysis would be precisely identical in every instance, and would lead us directly to the fear, the fury, and the struggle, the quickened and intensified life, aroused by the storm, which agitated the breast of the artist at the time of the conception of his work.

Words and colors are so universally familiar that all perceive more or less clearly, and feel more or less keenly, according to temperament, the artistic intention of poet and painter, however ignorant of the technical means used to embody it; but tone is to many so new and strange a medium of expression that they are susceptible only to the sensuous effect

2

of music, just as a savage would see only a blaze of color in a painting, and catch only the rhythmic jingle of a poem.

I have selected a simple incident in nature to illustrate my idea. A battle-field, a love-scene, a death-bed, a religious ceremony—any one of the thousand episodes of life which awake emotion and quicken imagination—might have been equally well chosen as furnishing inspiration to poet, painter, and musician. Oftener still, some purely subjective experience of the composer himself must be sought as the impulse which quickened his artistic activity to fruition, and will be found in his perfected work by those who have eyes to see and ears to hear.

This inner meaning is often vague, subtle, ethereal, a shadowy emanation from that mysterious under-world of consciousness, with which music deals more successfully and satisfactorily than any other language, and which, in fact, in its ultimate perfection of utterance, baffles every resource. It is this inner meaning which it is the duty and privilege of the artist or the teacher to discover and make plain to others by any and every possible means.

"What is expression in piano playing? and how shall I acquire it?" are perhaps the most frequent questions asked by all music students, and are certainly among the most important, to which the teacher is expected to give a ready, concise, and intelligible answer.

Expression in playing is precisely the same as in reading or declamation. It consists in making unmistakably clear to the listener, by means of the proper tone, emphasis, and inflection, the true meaning of a composition, whether musical or literary. The first essential step toward acquiring the ability to do this is to grasp clearly and feel vividly for oneself the meaning which is to be impressed upon others; to separate this meaning from the merely sensuous beauty of the medium and ornamental elaboration of the form in which it is embodied. To be able to express the significance of a composition, at least the pith of it, briefly and plainly in one's own words is always proof of this power already possessed to considerable extent, and practice in doing so will develop it amazingly. When a player has no more definite idea of a composition, and can give no more comprehensible description of it, than that it is a pretty piece, be sure that he or she does not understand its artistic import any more than if it were a poem in Choctaw, and will be equally unable to make others comprehend it.

The pupil should be led by easy stages, from the very beginning, to seek and recognize the intention and effect of every strain of music, even the simplest. In addition to the works he is himself studying, the teacher should frequently play for him short musical periods of a distinct but widely varied character, either improvised, or taken from compositions with which the pupil is unfamiliar; and then, by judicious questions, he should be trained to think and talk about the impressions so produced upon him. To tell, for instance, whether the music is fast or slow, major or minor, cheerful or sad, exciting or soothing; whether he thinks it would be suited for a wedding or a funeral, a hunt or a cradle song, a battle-field or a ball-room; to the bright, exhilarating hours of morning, the dreamy twilight of evening, or the gloom of winter midnight. Let him select an appropriate descriptive name for the strain, and in every possible way characterize it as a distinct entity in its appeal to his own nature.

Object lessons of this kind, continued and gradually increasing in comprehensiveness and delicacy of discrimination, supplemented by hints and suggestions from the teacher, by the study of writers on music and of the works of the best composers, will work wonders, even with the most unpromising pupils. I speak from experience, having tried the plan many times, and almost always with results as surprising as they are gratifying. The teacher will be astonished to find how much may be done in a few months, with bright pupils, in stimulating activity of feeling and fancy, in cultivating imagination and perception, and in establishing that instantaneous and sympathetic connection between the merely physical effect of music on the ear and the responsive echoes of thought and mood within, upon which connection music must base its only just claim to be called an art.

From this cultivation of perception and appreciation an improvement in interpretation follows as a matter of course. What is felt will be expressed the moment the pupil has the technical power of expression necessary, and there will be no more trouble from rushing a funeral march into a quickstep, or dragging a hunting gallop down to the amble of a tired cart-horse.

The tendency of this training, moreover, is to make better listeners, who are about as rare and as much needed in our concert-rooms as are good performers.

Six Easy Classics for Students.

LL intelligent teachers recognize the importance of familiarizing pupils with the names and works of the old masters. Not that these compositions are intrinsically any better than the best modern works, in fact many of them are really less interesting and musical and no whit better made.

But the old standard names carry a certain weight and dignity and the student's education is incomplete without some acquaintance with the old forms and methods of expression and the various stages of evolution through which the art of music has passed.

It is well to select a few of the best and most distinctively representative of these old, time-honored works, of moderate technical difficulty, insist on a careful study of them, and let them serve as landmarks in musical history in the memory of the pupil, as well as typical specimens of the forms and manner of musical thought in those earlier days. The permanent impression made upon the mind of the child by pieces of this kind is of utmost importance.

The first choice of half a dozen such works would most naturally include the following:

The Largo in G, by Handel.

This is a fine study in the production of a broad, sonorous, yet mellow tone in full chords, with a sustained melody which must be given special prominence, and also in a grave dignified style of playing seldom demanded by the modern works. The very term *largo*, which means large, broad, or in other words massive and very slow, is seldom seen now. Most of our modern music, like our manner of living, is too hurried and impetuous for such a style.

This composition is distinctly religious in character and should be given with a serious, almost devotional spirit. It suggests the vast dim aisles, the stately pillars, the lofty vaulted dome, of some solemn cathedral, where the reverential hush, and vague awe of bygone generations and dead ages seem to linger in the air like the faint odor of incense, and the lightest footfall echoes weirdly above the tombs of the forgotten dead.

The Harmonious Blacksmith, Handel.

This is decidedly the most famous of all Handel's works for the piano, was formerly in universal use, and still holds its own to some extent in popular favor, even appearing at times on the concert programs of prominent artists. It is a good study in clear, melodic phrasing, and crisp, clean-cut finger work.

It consists of a simple, cheerful theme with several increasingly difficult variations, a form once very much in vogue but now rather antiquated and seldom used. It is said to have been conceived under the following circumstances. Handel, who was living in England at the time, was on his way one summer afternoon to the chapel at Cannons to use the organ. He was caught in a sudden thunder shower and took temporary refuge in the village smithy. The sturdy, cheery smith was hard at work at his anvil and sang to himself as he worked, keeping time with the ringing rhythmic blows of the hammer.

This lusty, jovial song, to the fitting accompaniment of the hammer strokes on the iron, while the sparks flew in bright showers and the ruddy forge-fire glowed in the background, furnished Handel with the actual theme, as well as the general idea for this composition. This picture of simple village life and honest cheerful toil in old England should be borne clearly in mind by the player, and its mood reproduced in the music. Alas! for the hearty, healthy, happy yeoman of the old days whom it recalls! The type is well-nigh obsolete in our time.

The melody is supposed to be the song of the smith, note for note, as he sang it, and the suggestions of rhythmic hammer strokes, and clanging anvil, and flying sparks, are obvious and unmistakable. The atmosphere of the forge has been retained, but at the same time, medocrity has been avoided.

This work is a bit of avowed realism, though written at a time when descriptive music was supposed to be unknown or disdained.

The fact is that its beginnings are to be found even among the works of Handel, Haydn, and most of the other so-called severe classicists. Even Bach in his dance forms was pictorial.

The Loure in G, by Bach.

The Loure is an antique rustic dance originating in Normandy. It is somewhat slower than the jig and was named after the Loure, a local form of bag-pipe which usually furnished the music for the danc-ing. I have found this composition one of the most useful and practicable teaching pieces by this old, scholarly, ponderous giant in the realm of tone, whose very name is a terror to most pupils at first, but whom it is not possible or desirable to ignore in the study of the art in which he ranks as one of the greatest.

The involved, polyphonic style of music, appealing chiefly to the intellect and the sense of mathematical relation and proportion, so much in vogue in his time, and in which he immeasurably excelled all other writers of any age, is not attractive to most young students in the beginning. It demands more intelligent in-sight into form, more depth and gravity of thought and mood than they have at command, to be appre-ciated. It does not interest them and ought not to be expected to, because there is no developed faculty in them as yet which grasps or responds to it. We do not teach geometry in a kindergarten, neither should we try to cram a fugue into the immature brain of a musical infant, for a fugue is only a geomet-rical problem, interestingly worked out in tone.

The student's approach to these heavier, more com-plex forms, and the powerful, but somewhat ponderous, minds which produced them, should be gradual and

carefully guided.   Much is gained if the player's introduction to Bach can be made a pleasurable, rather
than a painful, experience; to be remembered with
affectionate reverence for the name and personality of
this new acquaintance, not with weariness and detes-
tation.

True education is the drawing out of latent capacity,
not stuffing in of unwelcome material by force.   We
enjoy and assimilate only what we can understand
at a given time, hence it seems to me wise to begin
the study of Bach with some of his lighter, more easily
grasped forms.

The "Loure" is a very old, now obsolete, rustic
dance, stately but cheerful and bright, full of the
lusty vigor and rude jollity of a simple, light-hearted
peasantry, accustomed to an active "out-of-doors"
life and to noisy, rough hilarity.   It is a little clumsy
and grotesque, perhaps, like an elephant dancing a
skirt dance, but all the more humorous for that, and
bold and brilliant and vivacious;   interesting to the
pupil and pleasing to an audience, which is always
gratified, in spite of its prejudices, if it finds that it
can really enjoy what is called classic music, after all.
This is a point worth considering by the progressive
teacher, as he finds that he must educate his public
as well as his pupils.

The Gipsy Rondo, by Haydn.

Probably no composition of the old school is so
universally known and used as the Gipsy Rondo.   It
is a stock piece in the repertory of every teacher, a

fine study in finger technic, a perfect specimen of the fully developed rondo form, and a bright, showy, pleasing number, attractive to all pupils, while bearing the magical name of classical music by a standard composer. "Old Papa Haydn," as he was called, with his good-natured optimism, his easy, cheerful melodious style, and his almost invariable adherence to the simpler major keys, with few of those objectionable accidentals, the bugbear of young players, has always been a favorite with teachers because he is a safe, conservative classic writer, and with pupils and their friends because he does not sound classical.

This best known of his small works is not, in any sense, a realistic imitation of gipsy music. It has none of the distinguishing characteristics of the music of that singular race; none of the strange melodic progressions, augmented seconds, and the like, and none of those wild, weird minor harmonies which are the ear-marks of their musical productions. But it is bright, spirited, full of life and verve, expressing the mood of the gipsy, as Haydn conceived it.

Imagine a gipsy camp, with the rude tents scattered here and there among the trees, a big cheerful fire blazing and crackling in the centre, and around it, in the flickering light and shifting shadows, a crowd of young gipsies bent on a frolic, dancing gaily to the music of fiddle and guitar.

The music should be given with dash and brilliancy, a clear, crisp tone and well-marked accents. Its underlying mood is that of joyous youth, unrestrained hilarity, and primitive, somewhat rough, out-of-door life. Its chief element of interest is a pronounced, pulse-stirring rhythm. It contains no hint of serious thought or profound emotion, only the joy of swift, free movement.

Sonata in C Major, by Mozart, Op. 112.

This much-used, much-abused, long-suffering little sonata, which generally serves the reluctant student as a study in rhythm and finger technic, and which is, of course, valuable along these lines, is nevertheless a musical gem, replete with fine ethereally beautiful melody and graceful embellishments. It is more than an étude, or a mere sample of the strict old sonata form. It represents Mozart at his best, expressing in a form as clear and finely finished as a delicate ivory carving, that mood of restful, sunny, impersonal optimism which is the essence of most of his musical creations.

It is like some finely wrought Greek idyl, the apotheosis of the pastoral, perfect in detail, without apparent effort, gently, tenderly emotional, without a trace of passionate intensity or restless agitation; the mood of a bright, cloudless June day on the upland pastures, where happy shepherds watch their peaceful flocks untroubled by the storm and stress, the vexing, unanswered questions and feverish longings of our modern life; a mood so foreign to the hearts and environments of most present-day human beings, that it is rarely understood by player or hearer and still more rarely enjoyed.

It seems flat, and insipid as tepid water, to the

fevered lips of the young, passion-driven, ambition-goaded soul in its first stormy period of struggle and achievement; but later, it is welcomed as the answer to that inarticulate, but ever increasingly frequent sigh for peace and tranquil beauty, and escape from futile strife, and vain seeking after lasting happiness.

The first movement gives us the pastoral scene complete; the green stretches of meadow, and summer breezes softly breathing among swaying grasses and clover-tops; the floating shadows of passing mist-wreaths across the azure sky, the silvery, flute-like notes of the shepherd's pipe, drifting through the sunlit spaces.

The second movement is like the song of the shepherd, tender but hopeful and contented, sure of his loving welcome when he wends his leisurely way back to his simple home in the valley as the twilight shadows fall. The last suggests the gay, but innocent frolic on the village green in the later evening. Throughout the entire movement one is continually impressed by Mozart's melodic inventiveness and inborn skill.

The whole is a musical picture of the simple life, lived in all sincerity by simple folk, not played at with labored affectation by the city-jaded modern victim of the relentless Juggernaut we call the higher civilization.

It is a backward glimpse into the heart of the golden age.

The work requires the utmost repose and tranquillity of style, an ethereal beauty of tone, soft and pure as the petals of a white rose, and an easy fluent technic.

Andante Favori, by Beethoven.

This work, now published separately, and popular, the world over, among all classes of players, was originally written as the slow movement in the great C major sonata, known as the *Waldstein*, also as the *Aurora* sonata, full description of which may be found in my volume of Descriptive Analyses.

As there stated, the whole work was dedicated to the Count Waldstein of Vienna, a descendant of the famous general and statesman Waldstein, or Wallenstein, who figured so prominently during the thirty years' war.

The work was composed as a tribute and with reference to the life, character, historical importance, and personal peculiarities of this great field-marshal who was, at the same time, one of the leading astrologers of his day.

The sonata was considered too long by the publishers, in fact was so, and is so still.

The Andante was cut out and published separately, and a brief, unimportant introduction to the Rondo substituted in its place.

The Andante deals with the astrological investigations and calm reflective mood of Wallenstein, the student of the heavens, rather than with the more active stirring episodes of his public life.

The opening theme portrays the quiet starry night with its hushed solemnity, its vast inspiring majesty and the deep reflective mood of the solitary beholder alone in his observatory.

Then follows a series of variations, or rather a progressive development of the theme, suggesting the growing, broadening current of thoughts induced by the sublime, the limitless host of inconceivably distant stars, gleaming through immeasurable spaces, the other planets, wheeling in silent splendor, all, as he fully believes, exercising an irresistible influence upon human life and destiny, including his own.

The heavier, more agitated octave passages later in the work, indicate his memories of the stormy, eventful hours in his own life, with their struggles and conflicts and victories or defeats, whose origin, significance, and ultimate outcome he is striving to discover from these mighty, inscrutable arbiters of his fate.

The close is eminently reflective, and its slow, hesitating, sorrow-fraught minor cadences show his longing for the ever-sought but never found solution of life's great problem, one more voice added to the volume of that great human chorus that, from all times and lands, comes echoing down the ages the same refrain; the old unanswered questions, How, and whence and why?

The true musician will render this work with extreme gravity, with serious, reverent, thoughtful tranquillity, yet with a certain repressed intensity.

Some Noted Compositions by Mendelssohn.

IT has come to be quite the fashion of late years, among a large class of musicians, to sneer at the piano compositions of Mendelssohn as shallow and superficial, and to relegate them more and more to oblivion; and not without a certain excuse.

His unvarying, blandly complacent optimism, his smoothly rounded periods, his graceful, but never profound ideas, and his occasional unblushing use of pleasing but century-old musical platitudes are all out of keeping with the intensity and complexity of modern thought and feeling and cannot but remind us of a very slender-waisted gentleman in full evening dress.

Compared with the vigor and variety, the uncompromising directness of the giant, Beethoven, or the fervid emotionality of Chopin, or the subtle mysticism and rugged force of the dual Schumann, Mendelssohn's style and prevalent mood suggest the perfect manners of the cultured man of the world, the social favorite, rather than the fine frenzy of that genius which to madness is allied.

But this very happy serenity and polished elegance constitute his peculiar charm and one which has its legitimate place and use in the realm of music and should not be ignored.

To some natures, and they are not few nor the most unworthy, all extreme emotion, which they are not so constituted as to share or even understand, seems unreal, hysterical, delirious, and its unveiled embodiment in art strikes them as indelicate, even vulgar; while to those more richly though perhaps less fortunately endowed emotionally, who demand in art the fullest, strongest possible expression of life as they know it, with its stress and strife, its tempests and conflicts, its unanswered questions and unsatisfied longings, even to these there come moments of lassitude when weary alike of the heights of fevered ecstasy and the depths of despair they sigh for the quiet valley of repose.   Moments when it seems better to give over the struggle and the protest, and drift smoothly on the stream of chance with shipped oars and slackened sails, with the will dozing beside the helm, and ambition gagged and fettered in the hold. To these, at such moments, and to the former class at all times, Haydn, Mozart, and Mendelssohn stand as the exponents of restful content, of delicate fancy, which pleasantly occupies without violently arousing the mind; of gentle moods, which lightly touch the surface of emotion as a swallow skims the sunlit lake without disturbing its darker depths; above all, of abstract beauty of form, of symmetry and finish, which gratifies the taste without exciting the feelings or arousing the intellect.

There are those who claim that this is the only *true music*, which is manifestly absurd. As well say that Wordsworth and Longfellow wrote the only true poetry. It is merely the expression of one of the infinitely varied phases of human life and experience—more or less persistent or recurrent according to individual temperament and circumstances. It is not the highest or the best, but it has its place and use, and the first duty of the musician is to learn to recognize and appreciate *all* forms and shades of experience as expressed in music, and to render them all with equal fidelity and sympathy.

An art which met only the needs of a certain limited class, or of certain special occasions, would be limited indeed!

As a study of pure musical form the compositions of Mendelssohn, especially his "Songs Without Words," are unequaled. Their symmetry is perfect, though simple, free from elaborate embellishment and confusing complexity—reminding one of the earlier Greek architecture, restful but satisfactory. Although these compositions are written in a great variety of rhythms and meters, and although the harmonies are distinctive and individual, they never lose the unforgetable Mendelssohn flavor.

His periods are clear-cut, definite and well-balanced, easily grasped by the student, and there are few episodical or parenthetical passages and almost *no* interpolated cadenzas to distract the attention from the general outline.

One may select almost at random any one of these wordless songs to illustrate to a class the distinct eight-measure period, with the thesis and antithesis.

3

The Spring Song.

This is probably the most famous of the "Songs Without Words," and is written in Mendelssohn's happiest vein.

The mood it expresses is thoroughly in keeping with his prevalent mental attitude—sunny, joyous and hopeful, full of love of life and a mild, pleasurable exhilaration. It was written in London on the first day of June, 1842, and is a perfect embodiment of the composer's impressions of an English spring, so well described by Browning in the lines:

Oh, to be in England now that April's there,
And whoever wakes in England sees, some morning unaware,
That the lowest boughs and the brushwood's sheaf
Round the elm-tree bole are in tiny leaf,
While the chaffinch sings on the orchard bough
In England—now!

And after April when May follows,
And the white-throat builds, and all the swallows!
Hark, where my blossomed pear tree in the hedge
Leans to the field and scatters on the clover
Blossoms and dew drops at the bent spray's edge—
That's the wise thrush: He sings each song twice over
Lest you should think he never could recapture
The first, fine, careless rapture!

The melody is a pure lyric suggesting a fresh young soprano voice, thrilling with exuberant gladness tuned to harmonious accord with the manifold voices of nature, wakening from their long winter silence in bubbling brooks, rustling leaves, and jubilant bird calls. Like the English skylark, it soars and floats in the upper air, pouring forth its overflowing delight in a shower of golden notes like sunbeams made audible.

The light rippling arpeggio chords of the accompaniment should simulate the swaying branches, nodding their cheery greeting to the passing breeze or the white fleecy clouds adrift upon an azure sky.

The whole composition is instinct with delicate grace, yet with a certain joyous freedom and abandon only fully appreciated "when the heart is young."

The Spinning Song.

One of the universal favorites is "The Spinning Song," a very clever bit of realism, as well as of tuneful melodic writing.

"The Spinning Song" has always been a familiar and much-used subject among piano composers, on account of the tempting facility with which the idea can be expressed on the piano and the variety of moods which may be coupled with it.

Every spinning song contains two distinct elements, the literal imitation of the buzz and hum of the spinning wheel in the accompaniment and the lyric melody representing the song of the maiden or matron who sings at her work.

This melody may vary in mood through all the gamut of feeling from rapture to despair, according to the emotional state of the supposed singer which it is intended to indicate. As, for example, in Schubert's "Gretchen at the Spinning Wheel," the heart of the singer is breaking, and every throb of anguish quivers through the song, while the very wheel drones sympathetically in the minor key. In this one by Mendelssohn the mood is quite the reverse—careless, light-hearted, with the sunshine of youth's morning brightening it. Fancy a young, sanguine peasant maiden sitting at her open cottage door on a bright May morning at her daily, but not irksome task, of spinning. The wheel hums and b-r-r-s at great speed under her supple, active foot, while her gay voice vies with the nesting robins in the blossoming apple or cherry outside, in a tripping lilt as light and free and joyous as the voice of the linnet, as fresh as the May breezes which toss the white blossom bells of the appleboughs till they scatter perfume music in sweet showers over all the country side.

The whole mood is as riotously gay as the May morning, as happy as the untried heart of innocence; a mood which we are the better and more cheerful to have shared—even though only for a moment.

The Hunting Song.

This is one of his brightest, most joyous compositions, thoroughly characteristic of his prevalent mood, and a fine piece of suggestive symbolic writing. It breathes the freshness and dewy aromatic fragrance of the woodland at daybreak, and expresses throughout the buoyancy and elation, the careless joy in life and action always naturally associated with a hunting scene.

One can feel in it the bounding pulses and superabundant vitality of youth and health, the stirring of the blood in answer to the voice of nature, the call of the wild.

It is singular that men are never so hilariously

gay as when starting out to inflict suffering and death upon their innocent brothers of the forest, who never did them any harm and are as fond of life as they. Think of a *man* with all the resources of his trained intelligence, supplemented by all the latest improvements in firearms, finding his keenest pleasure in mutilating and murdering a deer that has committed no wrong, and has no means of defense, no chance for life or retaliation in the unequal battle. To one who reflects, or feels, it is a fearful commentary on the cruelty and cowardice of the human race.

But that is an ethical rather than an artistic consideration, and has no place here. Art deals with life as it is, not with the ideal conception of what it might be.

As is usual in such works, the common device of imitating the hunting-horn in the theme or melody is employed in this work. The sound of the bugle or horn through the cool green aisles of the forest is always associated with the idea of the hunt. The various horn signals tell of the progress of the hunt, indicate that the game is *afoot*, or *in sight*, etc. In music the imitation of the horn is universally employed as the most suggestive, appropriate symbol of a hunting scene.

In this case it is not the shrill, aggressive English bugle, but the German Wald-horn (forest horn), an instrument of lower register and more mellow yet resonant quality of tone and Mendelssohn uses two, writing his horn melody in the form of a duet most of the time, and the rich sonorous theme rings through the forest glades. now stronger, now fainter, as the hunt winds nearer or further away. At the close we seem to linger by a bubbling woodland stream which gurgles and tinkles along its rocky bed, half hidden beneath a profusion of fern and brake, tangled elder and weeping-willow; while the music of the horn gradually recedes and at last dies in the distance. The ripple of the flowing water is distinctly given in the right hand accompaniment, while the receding horn theme in the left should be made markedly realistic.

The whole should be given at a moderate tempo, so that the ideas can be clearly expressed and easily grasped.

It is usually played much too fast. The power must vary constantly, and through a considerable range, to preserve the artistic illusion of the continuous change of location on the part of the huntsmen. The tempo ought to vary but little.

Mendelssohn was not a friend of the excessive rubato and it is not in place in his music. The *rubato* indicates agitation and emotional intensity, both foreign to his nature and style.

Venetian Gondola Song.   Opus 30, No. 6.

The Gondola forms an exception to any general characterization of Mendelssohn's usual style and mood. Far from expressing his ordinary cheerful easy-going optimism it is sad, even morbid, so much so that one is tempted to believe that it was not written by him.

It is well known that his sister, Fanny Mendelssohn, composed, and published under her brother's name, a number of songs and piano pieces now included among his works, as it was not considered "good form" for a lady of high social position to figure publicly as a composer—or in any other capacity—especially among the Jews.

It is not definitely known which of these works so originated. We are inclined, however, to attribute to her those of a more intense and passionate character than the majority, as her nature was far deeper and more emotional than that of her brother, and subject, at times, to moments of depression.

I fully believe that the work in question was written by her. This is indicated by its mood, and a certain vague indistinctiveness of form so different from Mendelssohn's usual clarity of outline.

In every gondola song and barcarole, just as in the spinning song, there are two distinct elements—the realistic element, suggesting the physical conditions on which the idea is based; the rocking of the boat, the rhythmic swing of the oar, the splash of water, etc., and the emotional element expressed in the song of the boatman, which may vary from transport to tragedy.

The gondola is exclusively associated with Venice, but it may be Venice smiling under the azure sky and glorious radiance of summer noon, or sulking in the dark phantom-shrouding fogs of late November. This picturesqueness appealed very strongly to the beauty-loving Mendelssohn.

The singer may be the happy lover serenading his promised bride, or the discarded and jealous suitor

waiting in the gloom of a murky midnight to assassi-
nate his rival.

In the case of this little work the mood of the singer
is that of dull, sadly pensive depression, discourage-
ment and profound sorrow; not new and keen, but
old and wearily familiar, sounding in every phrase.

The scene which forms its fitting background, is
Venice on a misty sullen evening in the autumn.
The sky and water are leaden grey, the outlines of
churches and palaces blurred by the heavy sluggish
masses of fog rolling in from the Adriatic. The boat
glides wearily onward like a spent sea-gull, rocking
slowly on the long tide-swells; the water whispers
darkly, in muffled monotone, of tragedies hidden in
its depths, with no cheerful splash or silvery ripple to
break the oppressive monotony, while the song of the
boatman, subdued and plaintive, voices in minor
melody the spirit of the night.

The very unusual mood here portrayed is exactly
duplicated by Edgar Allan Poe in the following lines
from "The City in the Sea":

> Relentlessly beneath the sky
> The melancholy waters lie,
> For no ripples curl, alas,
> Along that wilderness of glass.
> No swellings tell that winds may be
> Upon some far-off happier sea—
> No heavings hint that winds *have* been
> On seas less hideously serene.

Opus 53, No. 2.

Another of these little works, which it is more than
probable was written by Fanny Mendelssohn, and

which is one of the most beautiful in the collection, is the No. 2, Op. 53. It is a pure lyric with no realistic suggestion in it, dealing with emotion merely—an impassioned love-song, full of tenderness, fervor and ardent longing, with a marked undertone of impatience, uncertainty and restless agitation, expressed in the accompaniment by triplet chords, against even eighths, in the melody.

This rhythmic problem, so trying to the amateur pianist, of playing evenly and accurately two notes in one hand against three in the other, as presented in this work throughout its entire length, is a very important one and should be mastered early in the study of the piano; hence this composition, apart from its musical interest, is one of the most valuable and helpful of the "Songs Without Words" to both teacher and student.

The difficulties it presents are purely rhythmical, as the music is otherwise simple and easily understood, without any elaborate cadenzas or technical complexities.

The solution of the puzzle is easy when clearly comprehended, and once grasped, gives no further trouble. It is only necessary to divide the beat mentally into six equal parts, giving two to each note of the triplet and three to each even eighth, thus bringing the second of the *two* exactly half way between the second and third of the *three*. (At half past two by the accompaniment, so to speak.) That so few players are able to do this easily shows that they depend more upon the hands and good luck than upon the head. No student's training is complete without a careful study of this work. Having once thoroughly mastered it, he will always be able to play longer or shorter passages of *two* against *three* wherever they appear, without difficulty, and this rhythm is a common device with modern writers, to express unrest and agitation—emotional stress of any kind.

Consolation.

It would be impossible to pass from a consideration of these "Songs Without Words" without mention of "The Consolation" in E major, No. 9, probably the best known and most often played of any of the set. It is a fine study in sustained, smoothly connected chord playing, and in the production of a full, yet mellow quality of tone in full chords like that of the organ. Though technically simple and devoid of any very profound musical significance, it possesses a certain individual quiet charm which has endeared it to many hearts the world over.

It expresses simply and directly a tranquil resignation to the inevitable, a trustful, reposeful—almost hopeful—submission to a superior will and wisdom, which renders it restful and soothing to many minds in moments of lassitude amid the stress and struggle of life. It reminds one of the little verses which were so popular with a certain class of readers a few years ago:

> Be still, my soul, be still and sleep,
> The storm is raging on God's deep,
> *God's* deep, not thine, be still and sleep.

Be still, my soul, be still and sleep,
God's hand shall stay the tempest's sweep,
God's hand, not thine, be still and sleep.

Be still, my soul, be still and sleep,
God's heaven shall comfort those who weep,
God's heaven and *thine*. Be still and sleep.

The brief arpeggio passage used as introduction and
coda serves little purpose other than to establish the
tonality and make a beginning and ending. It is
wholly irrelevant, and might better have been omitted.

Il Duetto.

"Il Duetto" is a composition that explains itself.
It is intended to simulate a vocal duet between soprano
and tenor in the flowing, melodious Italian style. It
is attractive to pupils and is an excellent study in
melody playing, and dynamic values, and accurate
balance of parts; for the tenor theme must be brought
out distinctly, and carefully phrased, maintaining a
degree of independence, while remaining in the main
subordinate to the other. Both must stand out clearly,
with a warm, full, mellow quality of tone, suggesting
the human voice against the quiet, neutral background of the accompaniment, like embossed figures
in rich red gold on a soft azure field.

Why is it that these purely lyric effects in piano
playing, which form one of its most attractive and
beautiful features, are so neglected and so rarely
well given? Have we no time or taste for anything
but *hurry up* music, because we travel by express
train and do business by wire? Must we also have

our music ground out, machine-like, on high-speed gearing and served against time, like hash at a depot lunch counter? What wonder that our people have musical indigestion!

Prelude in E Minor.

One of the small works of Mendelssohn, which is far less known and used than it deserves to be, is the Prelude in E Minor, one of the strongest things he has done. It is a broad, vigorous, baritone melody, expressing courage, resolution, manly strength and noble purpose. It might be the musical introduction to the principal act in some heroic drama, in which truth, bravery and fidelity triumph over fraud and crime, winning final victory through suffering and struggle.

It is a thankful program number and a fine study in the production of a large, resolute melody tone, which suggests the quality and color of bronze from which the statues of heroes are made and predominates over a rapid, stormy accompaniment in a higher register. It is a good example of the *noble lyric*.

The Rondo Capriccioso.

This article would not be complete without a reference in closing to the Rondo Capriccioso, the most widely and favorably known of Mendelssohn's larger works for the piano. It is not of the first magnitude musically or technically, but is, nevertheless, a world-famous concert number, played by even the greatest artists, and very popular as a recital piece for advanced students in graduation programs, as it contains no insurmountable difficulties for the fairly equipped pianist and is always pleasing to an audience.

Its musical merit is characteristic of its author, and lies in its charm and grace rather than in any great strength or depth.

It may fairly be considered one of his best productions, and is full of quiet, tender, poetic sentiment and delicate grace.

The introductory movement, which should be played at a very moderate tempo, with a warm sustained tone, shows Mendelssohn at his best in the lyric vein and is more significant in content than most of his lyrics, while the bright, dainty, yet playful and sparkling rondo that follows manifests to the full his capricious, airy fancy, his happy, hopeful optimism.

Mendelssohn's best, most original work was on the style of depicting the half-playful, half-fanciful side of life and nature.

He was a tone painter who succeeded best in flower pieces rather than in scenes of battle or tempest; and he was especially happy in his occasional incursions into the realm of elves and fairies, as in the music to the "Midsummer Night's Dream," which was one of his earliest and most famous productions. This style is exemplified in the rondo movement referred to.

I have not been able to find any authentic historical. or even traditional, foundation for my idea, outside of the intrinsic quality of the music, but that is unequivocally suggestive. If called upon to give

a word-picture allegorically representing this composition I should do it somewhat after this fashion:
I imagine a long, gentle slope of velvet green meadow
rising gradually to a line of forest which forms the
darker background. The sun is slowly sinking in the
west, not in gorgeous flaming splendor triumphing
in his conquest over the broken flying host of thunder-
clouds, but gently drawing behind him the soft violet,
amber and pearl-gray curtains of his night pavilion,
as if seeking rest after his day's journey. As the
silence and the twilight deepen, the dainty little elves
emerge from the shadows of the forest and begin their
nightly dance and frolic upon the open meadow.

Occasionally, from the depths of the wood, can be
heard the good-night call of a bird, or a few distant
notes from the horn of a belated hunter wending
homeward.

As the sheltering darkness closes in, the dance of the
elves becomes more wild and unrestrained and their
fantastic pranks more daring.

At the close the first chill wind of night sweeps
through the tree-tops with a boisterous rush, and her
black wings fold over the scene. This is, at least,
as I conceive the work, though it is not ostensibly
"program music" and has no descriptive title to guide
the fancy.

Robert Schumann's Carnaval

SCENES MIGNONNES SUR 4 NOTES. (LITTLE
SCENES ON FOUR NOTES.)

MONG Schumann's larger works for the
piano, none is more frequently played,
or generally speaking so little enjoyed,
as the "Carnaval Scenes." This apparently contradictory statement may
readily be accounted for on the following grounds, and thereby incidentally
an important lesson learned.

The trained pianist finds this work thoroughly and
refreshingly Schumannesque, full of all the subtle
fancies, droll humor and originalities of treatment
peculiar to this composer; replete with all the kaleidoscopic variety of tone color and harmonic effect,
all the symbolic and realistic suggestiveness, characteristic of the romantic school, of which Schumann was one of the ablest and most enthusiastic
champions. Hence he finds it a fascinating study
and regards it as an effective number for the concert stage.

With the fatuous assumption, common to the specialist, that every one knows, or ought to know, about the subject-matter in question, he simply discharges this piece at the heads of his unoffending audience, on the hit-or-miss plan, in a series of fragments, like scrap-iron from a fast-firing machine gun, with the same rapidity and general inaccuracy of aim, fondly imagining that his hearers will catch them as they fly, and see and appreciate at a first fleeting glance that which has taken him, the professional musician, months of study to perceive and value properly.

The listeners, on the other hand, ignorant usually of the composer's meaning and intention, except that in some vague way the work probably has to do with a carnival, and often failing to comprehend the foreign names designating some of the sections, hear only a succession of incoherent, apparently irrelevant musical scraps, with no logical sequence, dramatic development or emotional continuity, without even a pause to show where one fragment ends and the next begins. They are confused, bored, and naturally conclude that if this is "high-class music artistically performed," they greatly prefer the kind Susie plays at home, with its marked dance rhythms and simple melodies, easily grasped and affording at least a sort of superficial sensuous pleasure; and it is no wonder they do.

An audience has some rights, and one of them is to know "what and where the player is at," to use a colloquialism.   Another is to get something in return for its money.

The following simple but accurate explanation may aid students and others who may chance to read it in arriving at this desirable state of pre-knowledge concerning the work in question. Some such analysis or description ought to be supplied, at least in outline, by every pianist who presents the composition, either by word of mouth or in print upon the program.

The secondary title, "Little Scenes on Four Notes," with its partial justification in the music, is based on a curious and very inadequately sustained conceit on the part of Schumann, namely, the use of the letters, A, E flat, C and B natural, as the initial theme in several of the numbers.

In English nomenclature this would spell nothing, but in German E flat is called es (pronounced S), and B natural is called H, so that the four letters, A-S-C-H, spell the name of the little village of Asch in Bohemia, the home of Fräulein Ernestine von Fricken, one of Schumann's most intimate lady friends at the time of composing this music (1834 and 1835). The same notes, S-C-H-A, also represent the only letters in Schumann's own name, which are used in musical notation, and he seems to have never tired of playing upon and with them in his compositions.

This form of musical joke, which consisted in cleverly working the letters of some proper name into the theme of a composition, was quite in vogue with musicians of Schumann's and preceding generations. Sebastian Bach was guilty of building his own name into a theme B-A-C-H, and Schumann employed the same device in his very first composition, his Op. 1, of which the theme is formed of the

4

letters A-B-E-G-G, spelling the last name of Meta Abegg, of Mannheim. He later used Gade's name, and the woman's name Beda in a similar way.

It is possible that Schumann originally intended all the numbers of the "Carnaval" to consist of some grouping of the musical notes represented by the letters in the name Asch, but these notes in that order appear only a few times as the opening phrase of the melody in some of the earlier sketches. The idea is not fully carried out even there, and is later abandoned altogether, so has little value or significance from a musical or any other standpoint. It is merely a droll passing whim.

The work, as a whole, is intended to express the moods and portray some of the scenes and characters of the Carnival masquerade and procession, common in all the Catholic European cities on Mardi Gras, and witnessed repeatedly by Schumann in Vienna in his early life. The spontaneity of the minute, the spirit of frolic, and the poetical undercurrent mark the "Carnaval" as a most original work.

The masquerade idea seems to have had a very strong hold upon Schumann, for three of his most notable and popular piano works are based upon it. Aside from this Carnaval, Op. 9, the Papillons, Op. 2, represents scenes and characters at a masked ball, and the Faschingsschwank, Op. 26, depicts the Viennese Carnival.

The work we are considering consists of twenty-two musical sketches, and I have numbered them here for convenient reference, though it is not so done in the printed score.

No. 1.   Preambule.   (Preamble.)

This first number is a musical introduction, supposed to be played by the band at the head of the
procession, expressing the mood of the time, with its
excitement and anticipation, its complete abandonment to hilarious gaiety and rollicking, often rough
fun.   It is followed by a representation of a number
of the maskers in the procession, interspersed with
typical incidents and an occasional band number.
For this composition depicts, not the masked ball on
the evening of Mardi Gras, but the street procession
which precedes it.

No. 2.   Pierrot.   (Clown.)

This is a name quite generally adopted throughout
Europe to designate a clown or tumbler of the old-
fashioned uncouth German type, a personification of
rough, clumsy Teutonic humor.   In this case he
heads the procession, stalking down the street, pre-
tending to be master of ceremonies, preserving a
wondrous pompous dignity and a ludicrous solemnity, but turning a sudden grotesque somerset or
handspring at frequent intervals, to the great amusement of the spectators.

The mood of farcical gravity and also the realistic
effect of the somerset are graphically portrayed in
the music, the latter occurring on the single notes
marked *forte* in the midst of *piano* passages.   These
should burst out so as to startle the listener and

instantly relapse into solemnity as does the circus clown.

No. 3.   Arlequin.   (Harlequin.)

This is another impersonation of the buffoon, a harlequin of the fantastic mercurial French type, dressed in a vivid striped costume of many colors. He carries in his hand a long whip, which he snaps occasionally in the faces of the bystanders, ostensibly to clear the street, but really to startle and annoy them, and create merriment at their expense.

This number should be as animated as the former was solemn, and the cracking of the whip is unmistakable, occurring in the first at.¹ third measure, and at intervals of every few measures afterward. It should be given very staccato, with a snapping accent on the sixteenth which precedes the rest.

No. 4.   Valse Noble.

This is another composition played by the band, somewhat more subdued and graceful than the introduction, presumably heard at a greater distance, but distinctly music in the carnival vein.

No. 5.   Eusebius.

This number and the one immediately following it, Florestan, are interesting creations of Schumann's own imagination. Here they are fictitious characters, supposed to be taking part in the procession, but the names are familiar to all students of his life and works during early manhood. One or the other is signed to a large number of his critiques and literary articles, and sometimes both together to his musical compositions, as in the case of the great Sonata, Op. II, which was "Dedicated to Clara, by Florestan and Eusebius."

Goethe's oft-quoted statement that two souls dwell in very breast was distinctly true of Schumann, who himself recognized the duplex personality under the two names referred to, which typify two different phases of his character and genius. Eusebius represents the poetic metaphysical side of his nature, the introspective impractical dreamer, the writer of delicate lyrics and involved mystical harmonies. It must be remembered that Schumann's representation of his dual personality is not confined to his musical compositions, but continually appeared in his writings as well.

No. 6. Florestan.

As suggested above, this was Schumann's own name for his sterner self. Florestan is just the reverse of Eusebius, bold, aggressive, turbulent, fighting with fierce joy for his ideals, fighting if necessary with a club, and yet with a certain rollicking gaiety which suggests the college boy out for a lark. Florestan was the organizer and leader of the *Davidsbündler* or hosts of David, who to quote his own words are "youths and men destined to slay all the Philistines, musical or otherwise."

No. 7.   Coquette.

This admirably suggestive sketch hardly needs analysis. The name tells the story. It embodies in a musical form, replete with dainty witchery and capricious archness, touched here and there with seductive tenderness, the familiar and famous coquette, fascinating but unreliable. Most composers have tried their hands first or last at depicting this type of the eternal feminine, under titles containing the words flirt, coquette, siren, Lorelei, witch, and the like, but I regard this as a peculiarly happy effort and one of the best examples of portrait painting in music which has been produced.

No. 8.   Replique.

This is merely a brief phrase, a sort of echo or reply to the blandishments of the foregoing.

No. 9.   Sphinxes.

This number can hardly have been intended to be played. It has no musical significance, but is a jest in the form of a riddle, addressed only to one who is reading the score. It is another of Schumann's good-natured but rather awkward drolleries. It contains no notes, but the parallel bars which take the place of them are seen on examination to occupy places on the staff corresponding to the four letters already referred to, upon which the "little scenes" are supposed to be built. The first represents the notes S-C-H-A, the letters from the name Schumann which occur in music. The second spells the word *Ach*, an interjection in German translated by our word Alas. The third is the name Asch, the village previously mentioned as the home town of an intimate friend.

No. 10.   Papillons.   (Butterflies.)

The music does not represent in any sense the light-winged vagrants of the summer field. It suggests rather a group of maskers dressed to represent butterflies, but forgetting their rôle in the excitement of the occasion and indulging in a good deal of noisy merriment. They pass quickly and vanish amid the crowd of revellers.

No. 11.   A. S. C. H.—S. C. H. A. Lettres Dansantes.   (Dancing Letters.)

Here we have another recurrence of the quaint conceit already referred to, a play upon the letters A. S. C. H. and S. C. H. A., which are here made to dance and tumble boisterously before us like veritable living entities, none too sober, or a species of roguish kobald whose antics are supposed to be very amusing. The idea is ingenious, but the actual musical effect not very satisfactory. In some modern pantomimes the idea has been presented on the stage with dancers holding huge letters.

No. 12.   Chiarina.

Chiara is the Italian for Clara, and Chiarina, the diminutive, was a favorite pet name of Schumann for Clara Wieck, the charming and gifted young artist, afterward famous the world over as Clara Schumann, to whom the composer was deeply attached from her fourteenth year, and to whom he was secretly betrothed at the time this work was written. He pays a delicate tribute to her charming personality in this dainty lyric. The melody consists of a little phrase of four notes, constantly reiterated, in different positions but with the same accent and inflection, so as to simulate the syllables of the name Chiarina.

No. 13.   Chopin.

The next character represented is the well-known composer Frederic Chopin, for whom Schumann felt and expressed profound admiration. He has here done an exceedingly clever bit of imitation of the Polish composer's most familiar and characteristic form of writing, viz., the Nocturne, in which Chopin excelled all other composers, and by means of which, in connection with his waltzes, he first became widely known to the musical world.

This number is an exquisite specimen of the Nocturne, a tender lyric melody with a certain plaintive undertone and a flowing arpeggio accompaniment. It might easily be mistaken for Chopin's own work, both as to general mood and details of construction. In fact, Chopin's personality seems manifested in it, which of course was the composer's intention.

No. 14.   Estrella.

Estrella was a romantic name applied by Schumann to Frl. Ernestine von Fricken, a gifted and attractive young lady residing at Asch, with whom the composer at the time of writing the Carnaval was on the closest terms of friendly intimacy. Her personality is indicated, as well as her participation in the masquerade, by this very winning bit of music.

No. 15.   Reconnaissance.
(Recognition.)

Schumann has endeavored in certain portions of this work to express not only the general mood of the Carnival time and some of the characters in the masquerade, but also special emotions and incidents connected with some of its phases.   In this case, for example, the music indicates the feeling of glad surprise arising from the recognition of two of the maskers of each other's identity, the sudden pleasure of coming in contact with the familiar personality of friend or lover in spite of the disguise, in the midst of the noisy, rollicking crowd.   Although bordering upon the impossible, Schumann has attempted to reflect a mood which only the most sensitive tone-poet would depict.

No. 16.   Pantalon et Colombine.

Pantalon is the harlequin of Italian comedy, a fantastically dressed buffoon, the distinguishing feature of whose costume is that trousers and stockings are all of one piece. The name is derived from the patron saint of Venice, Pantaleone, and is a common one among the Venetians. It is quite generally used by other Italians as a nickname for one of whom they wish to make sport, particularly if a Venetian. Colombine is the sweetheart of Pantalon, and the two characters figure largely in the pantomimes of all countries. We are to imagine them passing in this procession hand in hand.

It may seem to the player of this composition that Schumann has given quite too much time and prominence to the clown in various types. But any one who has lived through the Carnival season in one of the German Catholic cities knows by experience that the streets are full of masked clowns on Mardi Gras, even in broad daylight, and they form the favorite disguise in all processions and balls. It is difficult for one who has not experienced the Carnival spirit to appreciate the abandon and effervescence of the convivial crowds.

No. 17.   Valse Allemande.

Another number by the band, an old-fashioned German waltz, of a graceful but rather slow and stately character.

No. 18.   Paganini.

Here again Schumann has introduced and unmistakably identified the personality he wishes to
have pass before our mental vision, by means of
an ingenious imitation of one of the best-known and
distinctive characteristics of Paganini's style, both
as player and composer. This celebrated violinist
was noted throughout Europe as the superior of
all players of his time in technical mastery of his
instrument, but particularly in the special form of
technic known as staccato bowing. The startlingly
brilliant, almost demoniac, effects which he produced
along this line have never been equalled before or
since. Hence he is very naturally represented here
by a series of crisp intricate staccato passages for both
hands, not particularly melodious, but interesting,
original and strikingly characteristic.

No. 19.   Aveu.   (Avowal.)

Evidently an avowal of love, from the tender
pleading character of the music, made under cover
of the confusion and the concealment of the masks,
in what the Germans call "A solitude for two,"
which is nowhere more complete than in the midst
of a crowd where each is engrossed in his own amuse-
ments.

No. 20.   Promenade.

Again a musical fragment for the band, in the
mood and movement indicated by the name.

No. 21.   Pause.

The name implies a pause in the progress of the
procession, but the idea is not carried out in the
rather impetuous music so designated, and its pre-
cise significance is not clear.

No. 22.   Marche des Davidsbündler Contre les Philistins.
(March of the Hosts of David Against the Philistines.)

This final number is the longest and most pretentious of the work and demands special attention, as
it contains many and varied points of interest.   It is
a bold, dashing and at times humorous composition,
in an almost frivolously jolly mood, written in three-
four time, to which it is obviously impossible to
march, unless in a sort of hopping, halting fashion,
like a man with one leg longer than the other.   This
odd conceit has undoubtedly some humorous and
symbolic meaning, which however is not apparent, at
least to the writer.

The title of this number has a double significance.
The Philistines, as all know, were a people of Pales-
tine continually at war with the Jews.   King David
won signal victories over them and compelled them
to pay tribute to himself and his successors.

Again *Philister* or *Philistine* is a term which for
generations past has been contemptuously used by

the students of the German universities, to designate the townspeople and other outsiders felt to be antagonistic to the student life and spirit. It was retained by Schumann long after passing his college years, and has come to be very generally adopted by the "younger blood" among poets, musicians and artists, to denote conservatism and mediocrity. Perhaps Matthew Arnold has best summed up the feeling in the following sentence: "On the side of beauty and taste, vulgarity; on the side of morals and feeling, coarseness; on the side of mind and spirit, unintelligence; this is Philistinism."

The David in the title as used by Schumann is one of the allegorical personifications of which he was so fond. It represents Schumann's creative genius as champion of the romantic school of music. *Bündler* is the German word for band or company, from *Bund*, which means a league or union. It stands here, as in several other of his works, for a little band of faithful friends, adherents and allies of Schumann, who rallied under his leadership around the standard of Modern Romanticism and helped bear it forward to the victory which was later achieved.

The Philistines, as used by Schumann in his musical and literary works, were the enemies of the romantic movement, the opponents of progress, the conservative, somewhat pedantic advocates of the fast degenerating classical school. Against them Schumann and his associates waged perpetual warfare, and like King David, he ultimately compelled them to pay tribute to his own genius and to the dynasty of the Romantic School of Music. Hence the significance of the title March of the Davidites against the Philistines.

To emphasize the careless, irresponsible mood of the Davidites and their contempt for the conventions, traditions and critical standards of the Philistines, Schumann has woven into the march very cleverly a quaint old tune of the 17th century, known throughout Germany as the *Grossvatertanz* (Grand-father-dance), and a favorite college song at the German universities. It was also adopted in this country and is familiar to those whose memories reach back over half a century, sung to the following doggerel:

> Tim Doolan he dreamt that his father was dead,
> And his father he dreamt that Tim Doolan was dead,
> And Tim Doolan was dead
> And his father was dead
> And Tim Doolan he dreamt that his father was dead.

The accent and rhythm of these words exactly match those of the musical notes.

This old tune seems to have been a sort of battle-hymn or rallying cry of the Davidsbündler, and appears in several of Schumann's works. In this march he plays it with a real facetious gusto, passing it about from one hand to the other, now in playful staccato effects, now in big pompous octaves, always appearing in a new key when least expected. He seems to flaunt it deliberately in the faces of his shocked critics, in the spirit of pure fun and bravado. The march closes with a spirited finale like a joyous defiance hurled at the foe.

The "Carnival" as a whole presents Schumann's

genius, not in its most profound and strictly musical aspect, but in its flood-tide of youthful vivacity, of exuberant fancy and fertility of suggestive symbolism. It is best characterized by the German expression *Geistreich*, for which we have no English synonym, but which means rich in mentality.

The work is replete with graphic realism and recalls Schumann's own words of his earlier compositions: "At that time the *man* and the *musician* in me were always trying to speak at once."

Schumann's Fantasy Pieces, Opus 12.

MONG all composers there is none, with the possible exception of Chopin, who possesses such a remarkable and unmistakable individuality of style and such pronounced subjectivity in all his work as Robert Schumann. In spite of the manifold variety of his forms and diversity of his subjects, he is always Schumann, not by any possibility to be mistaken for anybody else, in any single period. Whether he is portraying the graceful flight of the butterfly or the grotesque pranks of the carnival clown, the dreams of a child or the stern ambition of a hero, a strain of his may be recognized anywhere without hesitation by any one at all familiar with his work.

This distinctive peculiarity of style is due mainly, though not wholly, to two leading characteristics: a plain, wholly unembellished, almost primitive intensity of emotional content, and a certain vagueness of expression, an indistinctness of outline in his periods, which renders them hard to grasp. It is the former that so endears him to musicians and the latter which is responsible for his unpopularity with the public.

He has all the typical German's force and depth, all his fondness for rugged, even if rough, directness and for calling things exactly by their right names, all his scorn of mere external refinements and graces; but on the other hand he has, more than all, the German's involved obscurity of expression, his fondness for shadowy mysticism, his inability to formulate with clearness.

His grandest visions of beauty are apparently seen "as through a glass, darkly." His thoughts seem at times too big for his musical vocabulary. Or rather perhaps his ideas are poured forth from the volcanic depths of his genius, in a molten state, too rapidly to solidify into separate forms; but intermingle, overlapping and blurring each other.

This defect, for a serious defect it unquestionably is, will always prevent Schumann's works from being universally understood and appreciated; but naturally it is less apparent in his shorter compositions.

Of these, the *Fantasy Pieces Op.* 12 are among the most effective and widely known. They are very varied in mood, full of the richest, most vivid fancy and striking originality, and clearer, more definite in form than the majority of Schumann's works.

Aufschwung.

The strongest of this set is the "Aufschwung," a powerful treatment in music of the idea of human ambition, mounting with irresistible, inherent strength toward the summits of fame and achievement, scorning obstacles, defying dangers, ignoring temptations.

5

and the soft allurements of easier paths; sweeping onward with the overwhelming force of a tidal wave toward its goal, grand but destructive in its might.

It is the same idea precisely that is so ably handled in Longfellow's famous poem *Excelsior*. The player should study that poem carefully in connection with this composition, and reproduce its thoughts and moods in the music; it is often a help to have it well read to an audience before playing the number in public.

The bold opening theme in B flat minor is the Excelsior cry of the poem, the enunciation of pride, courage, resolution, aspiration, yet of a stern sadness withal, for ambition is the avowed and deadly foe of happiness. Then follow successively, as in the poem, suggestions of the various difficulties, temptations and dangers that beset the upward path, the seductions of love, the allurements of home and rest, the peace and resignation proffered by religion, the growing terror of the ever darker and lonelier way, the warning,

> "Beware the pinetree's withered branch,
> Beware the awful avalanche."

But, as answer to each and all, comes the reiterated ringing shout, "Excelsior!"

This first theme should be given always with great strength and dignity, increasing in intensity with each repetition. It easily may be—and too often is—made trivial by excess of speed. The sections which follow must be treated with the utmost diversity of shading and tone coloring, each expressing its own particular mood and suggestion, while the superb

climax in chords, with the scale passages in the left
hand, should begin slowly and very softly and steadily,
increasing in power and speed to the final reiteration
of the first theme, like the threatening whisper, the
ominous approach and the deafening crash of the on-
coming avalanche.

This work is a fine concert number and an invaluable study in dynamic proportions and varied tone
qualities.   The name "Aufschwung" has no adequate
English synonym.   It has been improperly translated
"Soaring," and so appears in many editions.   But that
word fails entirely to convey the meaning of the original.   "Auf" means upward and "Schwung" signifies
swing or sweep, with the implied sense of great power
and weight, as of some heavy body in swift motion
with resistless momentum.   It might be applied to the
movement of a battleship under full headway, but
never to a bird.   Or, if we translate the title "Soaring" at all, it should be the bold, strong, majestic flight
of the eagle that we have in mind, not the joyous rise
of the skylark into the blue.

Des Abends.

The exquisite lyric, entitled *Des Abends* (Evening),
forms a beautiful and restful contrast to the *Aufschwung*, if played immediately after it.   This little
work, one of the most perfect of Schumann's productions, is just what its name implies, a delicate picture
in shades of violet and pearl.   It expresses but one
phase of emotional experience, the quiet, dreamy mood
of the twilight hour, with just a touch of wistful long-

ing, a hint of tenderness in it, faint memories of the stronger emotions of the day, like the soft, slowly fading tints in the western sky, when the glory of the sunset has departed, that linger for a time as faint echoes of that symphony of color, then merge into the shadows.

It is the hour and mood which idealists love and lovers idealize, which poets have sung in all ages, and which Schumann sings here in as true and flawless a strain as was ever penned. I never play it without thinking of the opening lines of Byron's "Parisina," which it so aptly fits.

> "It is the hour when from the boughs
>   The nightingale's high note is heard;
> It is the hour when lovers' vows
>   Seem sweet in every whispered word.
> And gentle winds and waters near
> Make music to the listening ear.
> Each flower the dews have lightly wet,
> And in the sky the stars are met,
> And on the wave is deeper blue,
> And on the leaf a browner hue;
> And in the heaven that clear obscure,
> So softly dark and darkly pure,
> Which follows the decline of day,
> As twilight melts beneath the moon away."

The composition should be given with the utmost tranquillity, with a gentle, caressing pressure touch, with little agitating rubato, and no intensity of inflection.

It has been claimed that the form chosen by Schumann in this work was unfortunate and metrically incorrect; that it should have been written in three-eight instead of two-eight measure, thus making plain eighth notes of the sustained melody and alternate six-

teenth rests and sixteenth notes in the lower voice.
This is a mistake. Schumann knew what he wanted
and how to produce it. Just that slightly swaying
effect of the triplet rhythm, if properly handled, and
the natural lessening of stress on the alternate melody
notes falling on unaccented parts of the measure, even
though the melody is, as it should be, distinctly sustained, add materially to the wavering, wistful charm
of the music. The triplet rhythm is there for a purpose. It must be just perceptibly indicated but by no
means emphasized. The ear must recognize it unconsciously without its being distinctly heard.

Traumeswirren.

Perhaps the most original, and certainly the most
technically difficult, of the group of "Fantasy Pieces"
is the *Traumeswirren*, which we might translate
"Dream Tangles" or "The Confusion of a Dream."
It is a fanciful attempt to portray in music the capricious vagaries of a bright and happy dream, in which
a host of dainty, fairy-like figures, all luminous color
and swift motion, appear and disappear, floating,
circling, flashing hither and thither, as in some playful
dance of the sprites.

The middle movement in chords brings a startling
contrast, slow, sombre and impressive. It seems to
indicate the moment when the sleeper half awakes
and gazes about his darkened room in vain search for
the bright visions that have haunted his slumbers.
But soon he realizes the situation and you can almost
hear him say to himself, "I've been dreaming." Then

he settles quietly back again and little by little the dream god reasserts his sway.

This is a fine study for the fourth and fifth fingers of the right hand, and as such may be used by students, but it requires extreme flexibility, delicacy and speed, to make it effective as a program number. In fact, it is one of the most difficult things of its size in all piano literature.

Warum?

The most famous and, in some respects, the best of this whole group is the *Warum?* (Why?) It is very brief, very intense, supremely beautiful and technically very easy; a lyric of the warm, impassioned type, expressing the question which the name implies, with an undertone of sorrowful pleading and restless longing, more fully and forcibly than is elsewhere to be found in music.

It was inspired by and written for and to his beloved Clara, in the days of alternate hope and doubt and torturing uncertainty before their engagement. In those early days Schumann was an obscure but aspiring student at Leipsic, and already a composer of promise, but no prominence as yet, and of most meagre income. Through his piano lessons of Prof. Wieck, then the leading teacher in Europe, and consequent intimacy in that family, he had fallen desperately in love with the Professor's daughter, Clara, who, though still very young, was already recognized as the first lady pianist of her time, and had won fame and success in all the musical centres of the old world. She

was an artist of prominence, he an unknown student, and quite naturally the proud father decidedly opposed his suit, though Clara seems to have favored it from the first. The marriage finally took place in 1840, after five years of love, courtship and struggle, during which period most of Schumann's leading pianoforte works, including the one in question, were written. He himself confesses that they reveal and depict much of the personal experiences and feelings of his long and agitated courtship.

So much is fact. The following legend is afloat concerning this particular composition, which seems to be borne out by the internal evidence of the music and has at least all the probabilities in its favor, though I cannot vouch for its accuracy. In any event the legend is an interesting one.

One evening Schumann, having been most rudely repulsed by the irate Professor, in fact, shown the door and requested not to re-enter it in most unequivocal terms, wandered away humiliated and disconsolate to one of the many beer saloons where students congregated. He sat him down in an obscure corner at a soiled, drink-stained table. A wine card lay before him, and soon he began to pencil lines on the back of it, later notes upon the lines, and there, amid those vulgar surroundings, this perfect gem of purest art was born. It is the questioning cry of a soul, conscious at once of its own power and future possibilities, and of its present pain and piteous helplessness, and is singularly free from the bitterness and anger that might have been expected under the circumstances. Next morning the card was sent to Clara,

as a protest and an appeal in language which she as
none other would understand.

Their marriage was an unusually happy one till
darkened by the great and growing shadow of his developing insanity and ended by the tragedy of his death.
The noble woman, who devotedly returned his affection, shared his life and labors, interpreted and edited
his works, finally lived to be chiefly known to fame,
not as Clara Wieck, the celebrated pianist, but as the
wife of the great composer, Robert Schumann.

Grillen.

One more of the set deserves special attention, the
Grillen, usually translated "Whims." It is, indeed,
a most whimsical, capricious composition, full of sur-
prises and abrupt contrasts, of odd harmonies, unex-
pected modulations and particularly of fantastic
rhythms.

The opening subject, in chords, with its startling,
seemingly misplaced accents, recalls the swing of the
gavotte and suggests a jolly but clumsy country dance,
while the exceptionally poetic and attractive trio
theme affords a most effective contrast, like the motive
of kobold and fairy.

The work as a whole, both in conception and execution, reminds us strongly of one of those fantastic
sketches by Hartmann, entitled "Dreams," much read
in Schumann's time, by which it was very possibly
suggested. I refer to the one in which a rather bombastic, would-be poet of that day, whose imperfect
verse showed a decided tendency to limp, was satirized

in the person of a particularly grotesque Earth-Giant, with one leg much shorter than the other, making his clumsy advances to the muse of poesy. The jocose humor of the conceit would readily appeal to Schumann, for though wholly lacking, as are all Germans, in the sparkle of true wit, he was quite given in certain moods to a sort of broad drollery.

Ende vom Lied.

The last of the series bears a somewhat curious title, *Ende vom Lied*, which we should translate the "End of the Song." This phrase is a common conversational idiom in Germany, signifying the close of a story or experience, just as "Once upon a time" is our stock phrase in English for beginning such. Indeed, anything brought to a finish, an anecdote, an argument, a yarn, a joke, is dismissed with the words, "and that is the end of the song."

One cannot help feeling that it would have been better in this case if the song had ended before this last verse had been written. For the composition so designated contains little of the originality and power usually so plentiful in Schumann's works, in fact, seems rather trivial and commonplace and is rarely played, with good reason.

Schumann's Novelletten.

IN the earlier part of the nineteenth century, a number of German writers of fiction of the romantic school, led by Paul Heise, inaugurated a new departure in the realm of national literature. It was their aim to condense into from fifty to a hundred pages all the salient points, all the force, interest, and dramatic effect of the full-length novel, omitting all needless detail and florid description, all mere "fine writing" so called, and to concentrate their efforts on the plot and movement of the story, and to portray the life and love, the thoughts, feelings, actions and personalities of their characters, in a few bold, broad, telling strokes.

This new product was named the *Novelle* or *Novelette*, meaning simply a miniature novel, and became very popular. It fell into line with the modern tendency toward concentration and epigrammatic brevity. It was the beginning of the flood of short stories with which our literary market is now well-nigh submerged. In spite of the thousands of inferior imitations which pass current too freely today, the form when well handled has much to recommend it.

Robert Schumann, who was one of the staunchest and ablest champions of the romantic school in mu-

sic, and an inveterate foe of the pedantry, prolixity,
and over-elaboration of the old formal school, was
quick to catch this new idea, to appreciate its many
advantages, and to adapt it to his own art. He
wrote nearly a score of *Novelletten* for the piano,
some of which are among his very best productions
for that instrument. In fact, it may be remarked
in passing that Schumann seems, to the present
writer, always most thoroughly at home, most completely master of himself and his resources, in the
smaller forms. His pronounced tendency toward vague
mysticism and inconsequential wandering into the nebu-
lous regions of thought has here less time and space to
manifest itself, while his grasp of logical sequence and
symmetrical relations seems more fully adequate than
it sometimes appears in works of larger proportion.

In these *Novelletten* his ideas are admirably bal-
anced and expressed with concise precision. In most
of them he has adhered strictly to the original conception, which was to embody clearly and forcefully
in small compass the simple elementary factors which
are the life and substance of every good story. That
is, the strong, bold, sometimes even rough, masculine
element, represented in fiction by the hero, and the
sweet, tender, graceful, feminine element, spoken of
so often in German as the "eternal feminine," and
personified in books in the heroine.

The striking contrasts in their natures, which,
nevertheless, blend into a happy artistic unity, their
transient strifes and differences, and final reconcilia-
tions, and the difficulties and struggles which they
meet along the path of true love, which we are told

never runs smoothly—these make up the details and fill in the picture. It is a brief, terse, vigorous sketch, without a single superfluous phrase or irrelevant ornament, manifesting a refreshing scorn of mere sensuous effect and technical display.

Novellette in F. Op. 21. No. 1.

The first Novellette, Op. 21, in F, is the best known and most used, and one of the most satisfactory. The stirring first subject, in chords and octaves, is in gavotte movement, and the character of the hero it suggests is that of a rugged German baron of the fighting half-brigand class, in solid plate mail, hacking his way to victory and love with a mighty two-handed sword, though with a genial heart and many sterling, manly qualities. To judge from the second subject, the heroine is a mild-eyed, domestically inclined Fräulein, loving and lovable, with a marked religious trend of mind.

Novellette in E. Op. 21. No. 7.

The No. 7, in E, is almost identical with the above in general style and form, but the characters are different. This time the hero is a dashing cavalier, with more polish, indeed with something of the "grand manner," but not less of courage and prowess, perhaps a knight of Charlemagne's court; while the lady is unmistakably a court dame, a good specimen of the "steel-engraving lady," refined, graceful, charming, with many a dainty air and winsome witchery, but a tender heart.

Novellette in F sharp minor.   Op. 21. No. 8.

The No. 8, in F sharp minor, which is undoubtedly the greatest of them all, is not so easily analyzed. The outlines are less clear and simple, and the content more complex and metaphysical. It contains much of mediæval mysticism, much of thwarted passion, of vain psychological struggle, and infinitely tender sadness and pleading, while I infer, from the close, that the end of the story was tragic.

Novellette in B minor.   Op. 99.

The Opus 99 contains a charming little Novellette but little known, yet very attractive. It differs from most of the others in being more delicate and fanciful, and containing less of the distinctly human element. Its first subject deals not with the story of love and life and struggle, but with sylvan solitudes and their imaginary denizens.

To quote Kullak: "It suggests the sprightly dance and frolic of forest elves about a secluded chapel."

The Trio gives us the organ and choir within the chapel, filling the quiet woodland twilight with rich, solemn harmonies, while the evening wind in the tree-tops murmurs Nature's dreamy obligato.   When the service is ended, the elves resume their dance, which they have suspended apparently to listen.

The above will serve as representative examples of the Schumann Novelletten and the general lines on which they should be understood and interpreted.

The Arabesque, by Schumann.

HE term Arabesque is derived from Arab and signifies like, or after the manner of, the Arabs. The peculiar form of art which it designates is a direct product of the Mohammedan religion and reached its highest development among the Moors, who were Mohammedans of Arab descent, but who settled in Morocco, and later conquered the greater part of Spain, attaining a high degree of civilization, for that period, during their occupation of that country. The Mohammedans were strictly forbidden by their sacred book, the Koran, to make any picture, or statue, or any sort of representation of any human or animal form, or any scene in nature.

They considered it sacrilegious to attempt to copy God's handiwork. Consequently they produced nothing along the line of plastic art.

The Moors were an imaginative, beauty-loving people with a strong instinct for artistic expression, and, handicapped by this restriction, were forced to develop along new lines and create a new form of art, which is known to the world as the Arabesque. The aim and effort of this form of art are to express or suggest ideas, moods and qualities in their abstract essence, by means of form symbolism. Movement and repose, strength and grace, majesty and charm, elation or depression, etc., are embodied by means of symbolic forms, possessing more or less intrinsic suggestiveness and becoming, with study and familiarity, a definite and intelligible medium of expression, like the audible symbols which form our spoken language.

The simple elements of this art are the straight and curved line, corresponding to the vowels and consonants of speech. These are combined into an infinite variety of complex designs and elaborate patterns like sentences and paragraphs, or the different lyric forms of poetry. The intelligent eye delights in following these intricate convolutions, in tracing the symmetry of proportion, the relation and correspondence of the different parts and in finding the subtle symbolic suggestion they contain. The effect produced, and the kind of pleasure derived, are similar to those found in architecture and based on the same principle, viz., the significance of mathematical relation, which Pythagoras declared to be the fundamental law of the universe. But in the Arabesque, only two dimensions are employed, while in architecture, three are used, and in painting the third is suggested by means of perspective.

In music the idea of duplicating the peculiar charm of the Arabesque has been occasionally used, the delicate interwoven tracery simulated in tonal effects. The best example is found in "The Arabesque for piano" by Schumann.

The first subject, which is decidedly the best and most characteristic, is inimitable in its airy grace, its smoothly flowing lines and warmly sensuous curves, as real as if drawn in visible outline instead of fluent sound.

If the dainty tracery on those wonderful friezes in the Alhambra could be dissolved in the fervid molten gold of that southern sunlight and transmuted into music, we might expect a similar result to that here produced by Schumann.

The second and third subjects of this work, which is in Rondo form, are less beautiful but not less suggestive. They are more vague in content and less clear and distinct in form, with a hint of oriental mysticism, and there are passages where the pattern seems broken or incomplete, as if the composer had in mind some beautiful piece of Arabesque work which had never been quite finished or was in part broken or defaced by the vandal hand of man or time. But these seeming imperfections add to the subtle fascination of the composition, as well as greatly to the difficulty of its interpretation.

The work demands a clear grasp of musical form, a light, fluent finger technic, and a touch like the fall of rose leaves.

Schumann's Nachtstück in
F Major.

THE term Nachtstück means literally night-piece and, like the Nocturne, a piece of music so designated, to justify its title, must deal with some mood, or scene, or incident associated with the night.

Strictly speaking, any scene or incident or emotion which might conceivably form part of a nocturnal experience, from a love-tryst to a murder, from a moonlight boat-ride to a tempest and shipwreck, might legitimately be used as the subject of a Nachtstück; but usually themes are chosen which are more commonly and naturally identified with the night, themes of a tranquil, reposeful character, of which the Serenade is the most frequent. This is the case with the composition referred to by Schumann. The music describes no scene or incident, is in no sense realistic, but embodies perfectly the mood of the summer night: a quiet, restful, gravely pensive mood, deep and solemn and mysterious as the dusky vault of heaven where the storm-winds sleep; broad and vast and impressive as the slumbering sea with its vague hint of limitless power in repose.

It is the mood of a great and noble human heart, with infinite capacities for tempestuous emotion but in its hour of restful introspective revery and finding a sympathetic environment and symbolic expression of its own solemn peace in the kindred silence of the summer night.

The mood is that so ably expressed in Goethe's famous, oft-quoted, and oft-misconstrued lines, which, in free translation might read:—"Above all summits there is peace. In the forest boughs stirs scarce a breath. Wait awhile, wanderer, thou too shalt rest;—in death."

The character of the harmonies suggests the rich, mellow effects of the organ. The rolled chords should be played throughout with quiet deliberation and a clinging legato touch and the pedal must be constantly and most judiciously used, so that the upper tones shall form a continuous, sustained, and smoothly flowing melody.

It is a fine study in tone quality and pedal effects; the latter forming the chief difficulty.

The Träumerei, by Schumann.

NO composition by Schumann, large or small, has attained the same universal popularity with the musical and unmusical public of all lands as the Träumerei.

It is one of the "Childhood Scenes for Piano" written for young players, but which, though technically easy, are, with very few exceptions, practically unusable for teaching purposes, being musically too subtle and abstruse to be understood, or felt, by children; for the musical intelligence, as well as the mechanical ability of students, has its limitations, which the wise teacher must take into consideration.

The Träumerei is an example in point. It is like some excellent little poems by Field and others; ostensibly written for children, but really appealing, and intended to appeal, to more adult minds. It requires a certain degree of maturity both of poetic perception and musical insight, to appreciate or render it. I do not believe it can be well played by any child under fifteen.

The name means revery. It represents not at all

the dream of one asleep, tho' the word is derived from *Traum*, which means a dream.

It is a dream in the poetic sense of a mind awake but tranquil and inclined to pensive revery. It is a "waking dream" of childhood in after years, rather than that of a child, with vague regret for its bygone, fleeting joys, and tolerant though half-smiling sympathy for its transient sorrows, seemingly trivial now, but very real and poignant at the time.

It recalls the mood of that wonderful mystical hour, when alone with the silent beauty and suggestive mystery of the summer night, we first dimly realized our own identity; our individual sentient existence, with its untried abilities for joy and suffering and achievement; the hour when with nascent self-consciousness we felt, rather than definitely thought, "I am I, and I am a part of this vast, beautiful, but secretly terrible nature around me"; an experience which comes to every intelligent human being soon or late, but is rarely put into words, and of which music affords the only full and fitting expression.

The Träumerei perfectly embodies this mood in its softest, least intense and most attractive aspect; a mood too introspective for the real child mind, but universally *felt*, though perhaps not intelligently analyzed by older listeners.

This is one secret of its world-wide popularity. There is, however, another which is, and must always remain, an art secret; that nameless, unanalyzable quality possessed by a few poems and compositions and by a few only, which is not to be had by seeking, by means of which they find at once, and unquestioned, the open door to all hearts; a welcome alike from the uncultivated and those of the most highly trained and fastidious taste.

Shall we say it is the happy blending in equal proportions, •of translucent simplicity, sensuous beauty, and emotional significance? This might hint at, but not really furnish the solution of the problem.

Many of the great composers have done their best to strike just this vein and produce music at once worthy and popular.

Most of them have signally failed, their music, in this line, pleasing neither the musical public nor the masses.

There are a few notable exceptions, of which one of the best is Schumann's Träumerei.

Schumann's Romance, in
F Sharp.

THIS Romance is, beyond question, the broadest and noblest lyric from Schumann's pen. It is as grave and deep as any Adagio by Beethoven, as warm and impassioned as any Nocturne by Chopin, a masterpiece in miniature, faultless in form and rich in content, without a single dry, uninteresting or superfluous measure.

It is technically easy and melodically clear and readily grasped by the student, except for a few measures in the climax, where in an outburst of passionate emotion it becomes, for a moment, wildly impetuous and a trifle incoherent, in the hands of an amateur.

It is the expression of a true and manly love, strong, profound and enduring, of which the beautiful and gifted Clara Wieck is the object, of course. She was Schumann's only and life-long passion. He is away from her in Vienna at the time, in the midst of the mad pranks and frantic, flippant hilarity of the Faschingsschwank, the local name for the Viennese

Carnival, portrayed by him in the first movement of his composition bearing this title; and the Romance seems like a grave protest against the foolish mocking spirit of the place and time, an outcry of the heart for the truer, deeper things of life, of which his love and his Clara are the truest and the deepest. It says to the jesters: "Whereto is all this noisy striving after a factitious gaiety, in which neither the brain nor the heart of a real man can take any part or pleasure? Love is the only thing worth while, and love is mine, strong and sure as the sun in the heavens, enduring as the everlasting hills, though clouded now by absence. I wait, and long and hunger, but am not dismayed or disconcerted, nor is my spirit in the least diverted from its true and ultimate goal by the meaningless madness of this wild rout."

It should be noted as significant that the melody is not in single notes, like the pleading tones of a lover's serenade to his doubtful mistress, but written throughout in the form of a full-voiced duet, with occasional bits of interweaving counterpoint, suggesting the complete blending and interdependent harmony of two united lives, so characteristic of his perfect union with his beloved Clara through all the later years, till fate ended the duet with cruel discord, shattering his reason and her happiness by a blow.

Those of us who were fortunate enough to know her personally, and hear her play this romance, and speak of him in the after years, can, in some measure, realize what her love and companionship meant to him.

Schumann's Cradle Song, in E Flat.

THE Cradle Song (German, *Schlummer Lied;* French, *Berceuse*), with its general theme of world-wide significance,—maternal love, watching and soothing the sleep of infancy,—and with its realistic suggestions of rocking cradle and lullaby melody, has always been a facile and fruitful subject for piano composers. There are few who have not utilized it with more or less success. The one by Schumann referred to is not a great work, either as regards ingenuity of structure, or depth and complexity of the moods it expresses. It is just a simple, straight-forward, unpretentious cradle song, for every-day household use, so to speak, containing neither technical difficulties nor musical subtleties beyond the grasp of the ordinary pupil, and hence the more valuable as a practical teaching piece.

The gentle, reposeful, swaying movement of the accompaniment clearly imitates the rocking of the cradle and is easily understood and maintained by the young player; while the melody is a tender, quietly beautiful lullaby-song, making no attempt to express even indirectly the stress and agitation, or the involved psychological problems of our modern emotional life. It might well be the nursery song of any modest, simple-hearted, German mother, whose mental and emotional horizon is bounded by the walls of her village home, and whose preferences, as well as duties, are summed up in the one ideal of selfless motherhood.

Who shall say that Schumann was altogether wrong in this conception of what the true cradle song should be?

It is a homelike picture, rather old fashioned, perhaps, but possibly more restful, if less piquant, than that of the modern ideal of maternity, which rocks the cradle absently with one hand, while it writes club papers on Hindu philosophy with the other.

At all events, the work is an excellent and helpful study in sustained melody playing, clear phrasing, and tranquillity of style.

The short middle movement, in the minor key, gives scope for a little more dramatic intensity, with its suggestion of the gathering darkness of the coming night, pressing close against the curtained windows, with its hint of secret fears and lurking dangers for the future of the little life, now so carefully guarded.

But it is only a passing thought, a brief vague terror of the unknown, soon submerged again in the soft, warm flood of love, which for that peaceful hour fills the universe for the heart of the young mother.

Schumann's Vogel als Prophet (Bird as Prophet).

THIS is one of Schumann's ethereally delicate and fancifully suggestive smaller numbers, decidedly the best of his "Forest Scenes," and a great favorite with concert pianists.

It combines in a rare degree the openly avowed realism of the modern descriptive school of composition, and the more subtly poetic romanticism of the earlier period of musical reformation, if one may so call that reaction and revolt from the old "cut-and-dried" traditions of form and subject, and the opening up of newer and richer fields of emotional expression, and wider liberty of fancy in musical creation, which took place in the last century.

Schumann, in this work, gives us, not only a most dainty and fascinating musical imitation of the twittering bubbling song of some forest warbler, perched high in the swaying branches and pouring out his little heart in liquid golden notes like audible sunshine, but goes a step further into the realm of mystical, imaginative suggestion, and imputes to this bird-music a deeper, double meaning, a subtler sig-

nificance of prophetic import, bearing on the life and
future of the listener.

It is not merely a bird that sings to us in joyous,
care-free, springtime rapture, it is the embodied spirit
of the ancient wisdom of the forest that, in this moment of present gladness, hints of coming change;
the slow but inevitable circle of the years, foretelling,
with prophetic voice, the deadly frost, the falling leaf,
the gathering gloom and silence of the winter nights,
when no flower shall bloom, no bird shall sing, and
warning the listening mortal that, for him also, tne
winter and the night must come, when joy, and love,
and life itself will be for him as a forgotten dream.

It was characteristic of Schumann, as in fact of
every profoundly poetic nature, to perceive this undertone of serious suggestion in every sight or sound
of nature, however seemingly joyous; to find in the
music of wind and wave, of bird and bubbling brook,
a half-hidden prophetic import, an underlying minor
tonality, so to speak, a throbbing pulse-beat of that
great heart of nature which, through all its transient
hours of deceptively tranquil happiness and its brief
fevered moments of ecstasy, still marks inexorably,
eternally, the time for that dead march toward
dissolution.

The idea is carried out perfectly in this composition. The rippling, melodious arpeggio effects of the
first subject unmistakably simulate the bird music.
The slower, more sombre and pathetic second subject
indicates the more serious vein of thought and the
dark prophetic meaning, perceived or imagined by the
listener to underlie the whole. The belief that birds

convey warnings and prophecies to mankind in their songs is older than history. There are constant references to it in the Nibelungen Lied and other ancient epics, and even our own American Indians often stated that "singing birds" told them of an approaching storm, a fire in the forest, or that a neighboring tribe was preparing to take the war path; so that Poe in his melancholy poem "The Raven," which he calls "prophet still, if bird or devil," and Schumann in this more cheerful composition, are but voicing in modern art this age-old superstition.

Some Familiar Compositions by Franz Liszt.

THERE are very few of Liszt's composi-
tions which are technically within the
possible reach of the average piano
student, none which may be called easy,
but there is a very limited group of
much prized, much used, well-nigh
threadbare works of this "wizard of the
piano" which forms a part of the working repertoire of
every teacher and serves to introduce the pupil to the
peculiar style and special technical difficulties common
to Liszt's productions.

As intimated, they are not *easy*.

Bülow once said, very aptly, of Liszt: "The rest of
us *overcome* difficulties, he never found any." As a
consequence he has little regard for the mechanical
limitations of other players.

But the works referred to are possible for advanced
students.

Soireé de Vienne No. 6.
Schubert-Liszt.

The name signifies evenings at Vienna, and the piece
is an elaborate setting for the piano, of one of a set of

simple, graceful, charmingly melodious waltzes by Schubert, once much in vogue in the aristocratic circles of that second Paris, as dance music.

These waltzes by Schubert, though simple and unpretentious in form, give fullest expression to the half coquettish, half tender mood of the dance in those early days when the waltz was young and still possessed the charm of novelty; also to the graceful, yet vivacious step and gliding, circling movement which they were written to accompany.

They are full, too, of dainty suggestions of those elegant Viennese drawing-rooms, the sparkle of lights and jewels, the fascination of bright costumes, of shifting, kaleidoscopic colors, of the flutter of laces and ribbons and the witchery of smiles and glances.

This particular waltz, in Liszt's arrangement for the piano, assumes the proportions not only of a full-developed and well-rounded concert solo, but also of a complete and quite elaborate picture of a ball-room scene, drawn with the distinct personality of at least two of the dancers clearly portrayed in the introduction, with its two strongly contrasting themes. The first, a pompous passage in octaves and chords, seems to present the lordly, self-important cavalier in all the splendor of uniform, gold lace and orders, an officer of the Imperial guard, perhaps, stalwart, stately, assertive, more than sufficiently impressed with his own dignity, and the honor he is conferring upon his prospective partner; while she, a dainty, exquisite Viennese belle, a thoroughly equipped coquette, fully mistress of herself and the situation, is symbolized in the airy, capricious second theme. The two pictures are as clearly drawn here in tone as they could be on canvas by a master painter, and the individuality of each and the marked contrast between them must be strongly emphasized by the player. Then comes the alluring but simple little waltz practically as Schubert wrote it, after which the waltz melody is repeated entire, but this time half disguised and greatly enhanced in beauty by a continuous series of delicate, intricate embellishments flowing around and among the notes of the melody, as light and transparent as a fall of the finest lace, or the sunlit spray of a fountain.

When played, the melody should remain distinct to the ear, with all its rhythm, accents and phrasing carefully preserved and apparent through the silvery ripple of the embellishments, like a fair face through the fluttering folds of a delicate veil. The effect, when properly produced, reminds one of that famous statue of the veiled bride, chiseled from a single block of marble, in which every line of the perfect form, every feature, and even shade of expression, of the lovely face is clearly visible through the fine meshes of the long flowing bridal veil which drapes the whole.

The composition closes with a clever Coda in which the waltz theme and the "*leit*" motive of the lady are both utilized, and which also includes one of the long, tricky, chromatic cadenzas, the despair of young players, so common in Liszt's works.

Liebes Traum, No. 3.   Liszt.

This is one of the very few original compositions by Liszt which are at all available for students, hence is especially valuable to the teacher.

It is one of a set of lyrics for the piano entitled "Liebes Träume" (love dreams), in which Liszt endeavored to express in this musical form—precisely as a poet might have done in a group of sonnets—his idea of the different kinds and phases of human love, as experienced by various individuals, or types, modified, in each case, by the divergencies of temperament, education and environment.

The No. 3 in A flat, which is the best known of the set, deals, according to Liszt's own statement, with the love of a mature man in the emotional vigor of his prime, a man familiar with life's vicissitudes, its struggles and disappointments, its transient joys and fleeting hopes; a man tempered in the fires of experience, hardened by the constant buffetings of fate, yet preserving through all, in the secret temple of his inmost heart, a clear and deathless votive flame on the altar of his ideals. He loves with all the strength of his being, intensely, profoundly, passionately, yet with a certain grave reserve, a stern, self-reliant dignity, a strong, restraining grip on himself, determined that the tidal wave of passion surging about him shall not overwhelm his will or disturb his mastery of the situation. This intense, ever-renewed struggle between the raging tide of emotion and the rock of dominant will is the fundamental idea of the work, its esoteric significance, so to speak, but is an element not always grasped by the casual listener.

Superficially considered, the composition is a love song without words, mainly for baritone voice, cast in the form of a serenade, with harp or guitar accompaniment.

In the last repetition of the melody, in the soprano register, is introduced the suggestion of the soothing, tranquilizing influence of the feminine element.

Twice in the course of the work the melody is interrupted by a brief interlude between the verses, as it would seem, giving us a fleeting glimpse of the physical environment, a hint of the summer night in which the singer stands—the summer night with its hush and mystery, its subtle perfumes and vague whisperings, its wavering shadows and half-revealing star-gleams and the sense of indefinite longing and expectancy, which are its very breath.

The work closes with a passage of soft, sweet, restful harmonies, a sigh of content in the final fruition of love's dream.

The player should avoid the common mistake of accenting the running notes of the accompaniment in *triplets* instead of in groups of *six* as intended, which destroys the effect and their proper rhythmic relation to the melody

Consolation No. 6.   Liszt.

This is an original composition from his pen, of moderate difficulty and possessing much simple melodic charm, which, by its grave, tranquil mood and earnest,

7

devotional spirit, appeals to many, especially those of a religious turn of mind. It is one—and probably the best one—of a set of piano pieces entitled "Consolations" which were written, with many other more pretentious works—all of a distinctly religious character—during a peculiar episode in Liszt's varied and erratic career.

In 1856, tired of the world, its cloying successes and pleasures, its exhausting, unsatisfying excitements and dissipations, and under the domination of religious enthusiasm—very genuine while it lasted—Liszt abandoned for a time his phenomenally brilliant artistic career before the public and retired into monastic seclusion of the most strict and rigorous type in the Vatican at Rome, where he was the honored guest of his holiness, the Pope, and for five years devoted himself to religious study, meditation, devotional exercises and the creation of serious compositions based upon religious themes, many of them texts or incidents from the Bible, others upon spiritual experiences of his own.

Some of his best original works date from this period. (It was at this time he received the title of Abbé.) The "Consolations" were written at that time. They are small, comparatively unimportant productions, but are of considerable intrinsic beauty and are interesting because of the peculiar conditions under which they were written and of the unusual spirit they embody. They are especially valuable to the student in that they afford a glimpse into that phase of the composer's life and experience.

The No. 6, which is the most familiar, expresses

a tranquil, contemplative twilight mood, the welcome repose of a soul that has found rest and peace in the Faith after the storms and struggles and feverish agitation of a strenuous and not wholly sinless life.

It contains certain hints and echoes of bygone tempests, of doubt and rage and questionings, but softened and subdued like the sound of a distant sea, sobbing itself to sleep in some sheltering cave as the hush of evening falls after a wild day of futile fury. But the idea which forms the keynote of the work is final and complete reconciliation.

Serenade. Schubert-Liszt.

Among Liszt's most valuable contributions to pianoforte literature may be classed his masterly arrangements, as piano solos, of a large number of Schubert's songs. Some of the most famous of these, like "Der Erlkönig,"* "Auf dem Wasser zu Singen," "Gretchen am Spinnrade" and others, are far beyond the reach of the student and only available for a concert pianist. But there are a few equally beautiful, though in a more quiet vein, which may be safely attempted by fourth and fifth grade pupils, and furnish excellent studies in tone production and phrasing.

First among these is to be mentioned Schubert's world-famous and immortally lovely "Serenade," every measure of which is replete with exquisite tenderness and idealized passion. It is a love-song of the warmest

* For full description see *Descriptive Analyses of Piano Works,* by same author.

yet purest type, which will speak to the hearts of all lovers in all lands and in every age as long as love endures and music remains its most perfect and appropriate language.

This will prove an invaluable study for all who recognize the fact that the imagination and the emotional capacity of the player must be developed as carefully as his muscles.

It cannot be too frequently repeated, or too strongly emphasized, that *three factors* go to the making of the artistic pianist—hands, head and heart; or, in other words, technic, intelligence and emotion.

This composition presents one serious difficulty to the young player, viz.: the old puzzling problem of playing two notes against three with smoothness and accuracy in adjusting the accompaniment to the melody. It is not continuous, but occurs occasionally all through it, which is more confusing; but it can be solved with careful and intelligent study and is good mental training—as much so as a problem in algebra.

Du Bist Die Ruh. Schubert-Liszt.

This is a charming and comparatively easy lyric from the same collection of Schubert's songs transcribed by Liszt. It also is a love song, but of a tender, reposeful character in which the beloved is apostrophized as the embodiment of rest and peace, the solace after pain, the calm after storm, the twilight dream of a quiet heaven after a day of earth's heat and hurry and fretting turmoil.

Both melody and accompanying harmonies are wonderfully expressive of this soothing, tranquil mood—the very essence of perfect trust and ideal devotion. It is singular that this exquisite little work is so seldom used. It should be familiar in every studio.

Evening Star. Wagner-Liszt.

Another beautiful love lyric which Liszt in his piano arrangement has made available for moderately advanced players is this "Evening Star" aria from Wagner's opera of *Tannhäuser*.

It is sung in the third act of the opera by Wolfram, a man of noble and self-sacrificing nature, who secretly and vainly loves Elizabeth, the heroine, who in turn, loves and is beloved by Tannhäuser, the knightly minstrel. Wolfram and Tannhäuser have previously taken part in the famous singing contest at the Wartburg, wherein each singer treats the great theme of love from a different standpoint, the various expressions of the same general idea making of this scene a profound psychological study, one of the ablest manifestations of Wagner's colossal genius.

In this "Evening Star" aria love is extolled as the highest and purest sentiment of the heart, enshrined within a sacred temple, remote from all selfish and earthly considerations; a self-forgetting, self-abasing reverential devotion, to be guarded and cherished with a sort of religious ecstacy.

The lady is symbolized by the bright but unattainable evening star, the guide and inspiration of the singer's existence.

The melody is for baritone voice, rich and full
and warm, but subdued and dignified, a wonderfully
accurate expression of the intended mood.

It is, of course, accompanied by the harp, as was
the case with all the songs of the minstrels or minne-
singers of that early time, and the harp effects are
simulated, or rather, literally reproduced, in the piano
accompaniment.

Rigoletto Fantasie.   Verdi-Liszt.

Every teacher knows the facile and rather cheap
possibilities for display afforded by this old—not to
say hackneyed number—once a great favorite in the
concert room.

Any girl in the fifth grade, with lively fingers and
a supple wrist, can scramble through the brilliant
runs and toss off the octave passages with which
this work is so lavishly decorated, in a manner to
tickle the fond vanity of admiring parents and friends
and to score a point for the technical training received from her professor, which appears to be in the
opinion of many the sole purpose for which such
pieces exist.

Nevertheless, in spite of the facility with which
it lends itself to such use—or misuse—the work is
not without real musical merit and beauty of its
own special sort, worthy the consideration of the
serious musician.

It is a fine specimen of a class of pianoforte works,
now practically obsolete, but very much in fashion
fifty years ago, namely, the fantasies on operatic airs,

scores of which were written and played by most of the leading pianists of that earlier day, and which held a high place in popular favor.

The plan of construction was simple, demanding some ingenuity, but very little creative ability. It was merely to select and combine several of the most attractive melodies in a given opera, to form a sort of idealized medley more or less cleverly elaborated and highly embellished, according to the ability of the compiler.

The general form of the work and character of the ornamentations had usually no reference to any dramatic development or logical sequence of ideas, the aim being merely to present a series of pleasing melodies, decorated with pianistic fireworks.

In the hands of Liszt, however, this class of composition, like all his transcriptions, received more than the usual care and finish. The melodies were better chosen and better arranged, with some regard for musical character and contrast. The harmonization was richer, fuller and more varied; the embellishments more significant and effective, the resources of the instrument more fully utilized, and the result was the production of something more nearly resembling a genuine art form.

The "Rigoletto Fantasie" is one of his best efforts in this line, and though its charm is somewhat superficial and sensuous, as must be admitted, it is real and lasting of its kind.

The work contains several fine bits of melody of the warm, emotional, Italian type, some telling cadenzas, and one superb climax at the close.

It is an effective concert number, possessing the much appreciated merit of showing for all, perhaps more than all, it is worth.

The opera of Rigoletto, one of the strongest productions of Verdi's prime, is founded on that thrillingly, pathetically tragic drama by Victor Hugo, "Le Roi s'amuse." The plot is intensely, though gruesomely interesting, but of questionable moral trend, as it exemplifies the triumphs of evil, and the useless, hopeless sacrifice of virtue and innocence.

Liszt has selected three of the most prominent and characteristic airs for the Fantasie in question: the pleading, seductive tenor air of the heartless, pleasure-loving duke; the recklessly rollicking contralto melody of the mirthfully vicious siren of the story, who is indirectly the cause of the final tragedy, and the impassioned soprano lament of the heartbroken heroine, ruined, forsaken, yet loving still with unreasoning devotion, who dies by the dagger of the hired assassin, a voluntary sacrifice to save her unworthy lover, whose place she secretly takes at the fatal moment when her father's just vengeance was about to be consummated; while the duke escapes, unconscious of his peril or her devotion, a flippant song on his lips.

These three representative and strongly contrasting melodies Liszt has ingeniously woven together, closing with a stirring climax in which the last two referred to are combined as in the final act of the opera.

To appreciate fully the mood of each and to realize the dramatic situation, the student should read the libretto—or better—the drama by Victor Hugo.

Compositions by Godard.

AMONG the best modern teaching pieces of excellent musical quality but moderate difficulty are those which Godard has contributed to the students' repertoire. Though possessing great originality and freshness, both in melody and harmonic treatment, which raise them far above the commonplace, and introducing many startling and novel effects, they do not, for the most part, belong to the ultra-realistic modern French school, but to a somewhat earlier style of composition, in which the element of tuneful melody still predominates. Despite his occasional digressions into the realm of the fantastic, Godard may be said to be one of the few who, to use the words of a Boston critic, "still remember that the piano was once considered a musical instrument."

Second Mazurka. Godard.

His "Second Mazurka" is probably the best known and most widely used of all his compositions, and though rather hackneyed to-day, will long remain a stock selection in the class-room and in pupils' recital work. If well given it is always an interesting and effective number. It contains some rather puzzling rhythmic problems for the student, a number of warm, sensuous, attractive melodies, many rich and vivid harmonic combinations, and is a fine study in tone quality and contrast; the middle movement in octaves and chords affords opportunity for arousing the dormant fire and energy of the sleepy, lackadaisical pupil, who is inclined to play everything as if all music were or ought to be a slumber song.

The Mazurka is the characteristic local dance of the Masures or Masurvians, as they are sometimes called, the peasants of one of the former provinces of Poland. It is a graceful, languorous, coquettish dance, considerably slower than the waltz, but with occasional sudden outbursts of fierce Slavonic fire and passion, its distinguishing feature being that the accent falls, generally speaking, on the second beat of the measure. This should be kept in mind by the player and this rhythmic peculiarity made apparent, also the sudden marked contrasts of mood.

Music owes to Poland two of its finest, most versatile and dignified dance forms, perhaps more susceptible of truly musical treatment than any of the others, the Polonaise and the Mazurka. Both are most admirably exemplified in the works of the leading Polish composer, Chopin. The Polonaise may be conceived as representing the masculine Polish type, and the Mazurka the feminine. The Polish ladies are renowned for grace, charm, tenderness, fire and fascination, beyond any other women of Europe, and these are all found in the Mazurka. Liszt was greatly enamored of the Polish Mazurka as danced by the Polish ladies, and much picturesque language concerning it may be found in his little work on Chopin, which should be read by all who would understand the true mood and meaning of the Mazurka as seen "on its native heath."

Au Matin. Godard.

Another number of Godard, also well known, which no well-equipped teacher can afford to ignore, is the "Au Matin" (To the Morning). This is technically easier than the "Second Mazurka," but musically of a higher grade, as finely finished a bit of graceful lyric as can be found on the music shelves.

The introductory measures simulate very literally the distant chimes of matin bells, ringing in the new day. Their soft notes sound far and clear through the hush of dawn, and seem like an answer from the pulsing strings of the great harp of Nature to the touch of Aurora's rosy fingers. These measures should be taken very slowly and *ad libitum*, the sustained B flat being allowed to vibrate as long as it will, then fade away into silence, like a distant bell, while the changing harmonies below it are kept very subdued.

Then the whole composition, with its dainty swing, its sweet dreamy melody, its soft, warm, harmonic coloring, should be made to suggest the freshness, the tender yet radiant beauty of the summer morning, with the gentle sway of branches in the light and newly awakened breeze, the joyous bird notes welcoming the growing golden light. It should tell, like those exquisite lines of Lucy Larcom, of—

> "The grace of the bending grasses,
>   The flush of the dawn-lit sky,
> The scent that lingers and passes,
>   When the loitering wind goes by."

At the Spinning Wheel. Op. 85.

An excellent study in finger technic and at the same time in sustained melody is Godard's "At the Spinning Wheel," which, though not much used, is an effective recital number.

Here we find the usual device, a literal imitation of the sound of the spinning wheel, in the accompaniment, and above it the song of the spinning maiden, who is evidently in a mournful mood. The song is plaintive and pathetic, now tearful, now rebellious, but always with an undertone of impatient questioning of fate, of restless longing and half-suppressed pain. We wish we might know the personal history of the singer. This form of composition is always interesting to an audience, because easily comprehended. The realistic in music appeals far more to the average listener than the emotional or the symbolic, because more readily grasped.

Cavalier Fantastique.   Godard.

One of the strongest things from Godard's pen, a work very different from the foregoing, broad, heavy, dramatic and a fine study in chords and octave playing, is the "Cavalier Fantastique." This is one of his departures into the fantastic referred to, but for all that a most original and fascinating number.

It represents a knight of the olden times, disappointed in love or defeated at arms, desperate, reckless, vengeful, pounding away at headlong gallop on his heavily armored charger, across the echoing drawbridge and down the steep, stony bridle-path from the great forbidding feudal stronghold that looms dark behind him, away into the chill and gloom of a winter night, away and ever away, into a world that holds no joy, no hope, no definite purpose for him, but to escape what lies behind, his heart in a flame, his brain in a tumult of frenzied rage. It is a study in black, shot with lurid flashes of passion and a masterpiece of its kind. It must be given with limitless dash and abandon, and a firm dramatic quality of tone verging, toward the close, on the harsh and strident. Though short, it taxes to the limit the strength and endurance of the player.

L'Indienne, by Godard.

NE of the strongest, most strikingly original compositions in Godard's "Magic Lantern" series, is entitled "L'Indienne" (The Indian). It will never become generally popular on account of its peculiar form and its very unusual mood; but it is, for these very reasons, of great and novel interest to musicians. It was suggested by a remarkably strange and powerful picture, bearing the same title, by a painter, whose name I have, unfortunately, forgotten and cannot now find, which was exhibited in a number of galleries some years ago.

The scene is a giant forest, of a sombre and forbidding aspect, writhing in the torturing grip of a furious tempest. The great branches bend and twist and entwine as if in acute agony. The beholder can almost hear them moaning and shrieking in their pain. The monster trunks reel and shiver in the shock of the blast. The whole vivid impression is one of fierce turmoil and almost supernatural terror.

Two figures in the foreground give the needed touch of human interest to the scene, and the almost violent contrast of an immovable calm in the midst of that wild agitation—one in the stillness of death, the other in that of frozen despair. At the foot of one of the mammoth trees a beautiful Indian girl lies dead on a rude bier. Above her a stalwart young brave, in full war paint and feathers, stands motionless, with folded arms, gazing down, in wordless, tearless sorrow on the fair, still face of her who was evidently his bride.

The wind plays mad pranks with his fluttering garments and streaming hair, threatening to tear them from his body; but he neither heeds nor knows it, absorbed in his mighty struggle with this strong, unfamiliar foe, a great grief, which grips him cruelly, but shall not wring from the proud warrior the smallest sign of weakness. His face is sternly set, his pose is that of a bronze statue, indifferent to passing time or outward conditions. The whole conception is gloomily grand, almost sinister in its ominous repose of suppressed passion.

Godard's music faithfully and forcefully reproduces this impression of silent, sullen grief, of subdued power, of gloomy, hopeless, but uncomplaining loneliness; of elemental rage, met by passive resistance, by proud stoicism. The first theme, with its sombre setting, portrays the personality and mood of the warrior; and, at its repetition later, the storm effects are introduced with startling realism. The composition will prove of exceptional interest to those who are in search of novel impressions in music, and to whom the dramatic element in tonal art appeals more strongly than mere sensuous beauty.

Trilby, by Godard.

HIS is a most interesting, fanciful and strikingly descriptive sketch for the piano, by one of the best modern French composers, and an excellent example of the realistic French School of Composition of the present day. It is very little used, indeed hardly even known, in this country, but will be found to be a valuable study and a grateful and attractive concert number, presenting a variety of strongly contrasting effects, some of which are most novel and original, and appealing forcefully to the imagination of player and listener.

The name "Trilby" is somewhat misleading to most American readers—suggesting at once the story of Trilby by Du Maurier, which was so universally read and generally popular in this country some years ago, but with which this composition has absolutely no connection, beyond a chance similarity of name.

The legend of Trilby, with which it deals and which may be found best told in the exquisitely poetic French prose of Charles Gautier, where Godard derived his subject and inspiration, is, briefly outlined, as follows:

Trilby, the fantastic little hero of the story, was a

fire-sprite, who dwelt in the cozy chimney nook in a fisherman's cottage, on the shore of a Highland loch in Scotland, back in that vaguely indefinite period conveniently designated by the romancers, as "once upon a time." He wore a variegated Tartan plaid of deftly woven flames, and a jaunty little cap of blue smoke, and used to dance and frolic amid the flying sparks and cheery crackle of the fire, dance his best and prettiest, and play his winsome or mischievous pranks about the room to attract the attention of the fisherman's fair daughter, who sat by the evening fire to spin.

Poor little Trilby, mere sprite though he was, and a very small sprite at that, was very much in love with the fisherman's daughter and did his best to win her favor. But she cared little enough for him. An amused smile, such as one gives to the pretty antics of a kitten, or a half-playful scolding when he tangled her thread, or unfastened and let down her hair, in a teasing mood, was the most she would ever accord him, then relapse into her fireside dreams of more serious things, perchance of some mortal lover. Then Trilby, in despair, would give up his dancing and try singing to her a quaint, weird, but plaintive little love song of Spriteland origin, while the green back-log hummed a low accompaniment, and his brothers, the sparks, kept time with their little clattering castanets. But the song serves his purpose less than the dance, for it harmonizes with her grave thoughts, and but charms her into deeper reverie, so he returns to his dancing.

At last, his long awaited opportunity comes, as he

8

thinks, to be of real service to her and insure her gratitude. Her father being away at a distant town, she must herself attend to the fishing nets spread in the lake near by. So she looses the skiff from its moorings and puts off; but is hardly well afloat before she is caught in one of those sudden violent mountain tempests, so common to the Highlands, which come swooping down from the peaks above like a black bird of prey, shadowing the little loch with its wings of darkness, and arousing echoes, that lie like wakeful watch-dogs among the crags and cliffs around, to furious answering chorus, with crash of thunder and shriek of storm-wind and war of angry waves.

Alone in her tossing skiff, at the mercy of wind and wave, bewildered by the alternate gloom and lightning glare, our heroine was in imminent danger, when little Trilby comes gallantly to the rescue, in the guise of a will o' the wisp; still in keeping with his character, he dances across the foaming billows to her side, gives her the much needed light and half guides, half draws the boat back to its moorings, and she is saved. Then he accompanies her back to the cottage, singing again his pathetic little love song, while the storm, its brief fury spent, recedes into the distance, the mutterings of its baffled rage dying away behind the encircling hills.

Trilby now expects gratitude, if not affection. But no. Again he is to be disappointed. She thinks that, being a sprite, he has control of the elements, and that the storm is only one of his tricks, called up especially to frighten her, and give himself the chance for seemingly heroic rescue, for the purpose of securing her gratitude. She is very indignant and vows that she will endure his persecution no longer. So she goes at once for the good priest of the district, who soon comes with his sacred book and symbols, his muttered formulas and his cruel holy-water, and exorcises poor little Trilby from his safe cozy nook in the warm chimney, and drives him out into the cold, dark forest, where he dies of damp and chill and loneliness.

This composition treats the story in three distinct and very realistic movements. First, the dance among the flames, spritely, sparkling, piquant, yet dainty and fantastic, which is twice repeated. Second, the love song, full of novel, fascinating and plaintive beauty, and the more odd and uncanny, for being written in five-four time, one of the very few really artistic and musical examples of this extremely unusual rhythm in piano literature. Third, the tempest, brief but exceedingly strong and graphic, with its most realistic thunder, its shuddering chromatic progressions, veritably darkness made audible, and its ominous receding whisper at the close, like threats of future vengeance. Trilby's last, short, flurried, terrified attempt to repeat his old fire-dance before he is relentlessly driven off up the chimney, is touching in its half pathetic, half humorous suggestiveness.

The whole is fanciful in the extreme and admirably in keeping with the playful, tender mood of the legend as given in the French version of M. Gautier.

Pan's Flute, by Godard

THIS is a small but daintily exquisite composition, cleverly embodying the idea suggested by the name. Pan, it will be remembered, was the Greek god of Nature, the special divinity of field and forest, of pastoral life and rustic scenes and pleasures. He was also, according to Greek mythology, the inventor of the flute, or shepherd's pipe, and the first of the world's great players upon this typically pastoral instrument. Hence the frequent references to the pipe of Pan, so familiar to readers of classic literature. He was supposed to be specially enamored of the nymph, "Echo," the most coy and unapproachable of all the fair denizens of mountain and forest, and it is intimated that her fondness for sweet sounds and readiness to respond to them first gave him the idea and incentive for the devising of this instrument, by means of which he might, like the birds, do his wooing in melody. This little composition purports to be one of Pan's capricious improvisations; the accompaniment, in slow, reposeful, yet sonorous chords, soft but rich, and of very ingenious harmonic texture, symbolizes the forest, on the edge of which we may fancy him standing,

just at evening, gazing across toward the hillside home
of his beloved Echo; the forest, with its dark, restful
depths, its dreaming shadows and the occasional
organ-like swell of its solemn voice when stirred in its
slumber by the passing wind.   Above this accompaniment, delicate, but distinct in the right hand, Pan's
flute piping its dainty pastoral melody, fitfully at first,
as if experimenting with his new-found instrument
in various keys and registers; then, in fuller, swifter
cadences, as assurance grows and with it the desire
to win an answer from the faint, sweet voice so fondly
awaited.   In this he would seem, in a measure, successful, as hinted by the soft, reiterated, echo-like sequences
at the close.

In this connection I have a suggestion to make to
the many earnest, conscientious teachers in small
communities, struggling patiently with a class of not
overly well-endowed pupils, who have had few advantages for general musical culture, and with a busy,
superficial and rather indifferent public.

Plan a series of informal pupils' recitals, with brief
programs, each devoted to some particular composer.
Now do not, in a frenzy of enthusiasm for educating
the public, begin with an entire program of Bach
fugues, to be followed the next week by five Beethoven
sonatas, administered without a word of enlighten-
ment.   If you do, your audience will not survive to the
third meeting; your course will come to an untimely
end, and you will not have accomplished your purpose, but will instead have given your patrons a practical demonstration of their own previously vague
theories that classical music is always a bore.

Select some always standard and meritorious but rather comprehensible and melodic composer, like Godard. Take, for instance, six of the compositions enumerated above and give them in the following order: 1, The Mazurka; 2, Au Matin; 3, Spinning Song; 4, Trilby; 5, Pan's Flute; 6, Cavalier Fantastique. Write yourself a brief, but graphic and interesting, sketch of the composer and his work, which you will either read yourself as prelude to the program, or have read by some pupil who has a pleasant voice, good enunciation and intelligent delivery. Then precede each of the selections rendered by the pupils with a short description such as I have written, or other and better ones if you have them at hand.

You will find such a lecture-recital much more of a success with your audience than the ordinary miscellaneous, incoherent, indigestible pupils' program. Give such recitals as often as you yourself can prepare the sketches and your pupils the pieces, presenting a new composer each time. In this way you will do much to arouse the interest and enthusiasm of your students and to keep them at their practice faithfully, and you will find that you have insinuated unawares into your public much information concerning pianoforte literature and many miscellaneous musical ideas. Occasionally you will have the satisfaction of awakening a taste for music and love of it hitherto dormant. All of which makes for general musical culture in a community, and lightens the labors and increases the success of the music teacher.

Schytté's Compositions as Teaching Material

MONG the romantic composers of the present day, or the recent past, none offers to the musical world a richer, more varied selection of genuinely meritorious small compositions, available for teaching purposes, than Schytté.

Though Scandinavian by birth and early education, he has none of the distinctively Norse characteristics so pronounced in Grieg; none of the weird, grotesque suggestions of winter-midnight dreams of troll and werewolf, which one might expect to find in his music as a sort of racial birthmark; neither has he the striking, bizarre originality and odd piquancy of his popular French contemporary, Godard; but he has more breadth and versatility, more melodic spontaneity than either.

Like that of Rubinstein, his music may be said to be cosmopolitan, rather than national or strongly individual.

His family is said to have originally come from Finland. The Finns are of pure, though very early,

Aryan stock, a division of that race which began its migrations even prior to the Celts, but resembling them more nearly than they do the Teutons or the Slavs.

This fact, if it be such, coupled with his thorough German musical training, would account for the lack of Norse traits in his productions, as also for the notable leaning toward the fairly conservative German school in his work.

Nevertheless, his creations, though neither vividly local in color nor narrowly personal in tone, possess an originality and freshness all their own and show a mastery of form and a command of melodic and harmonic material manifested by few modern writers.

The following—selected from among his easier things —will be found of special interest to the teacher.

At Evening. Schytté.

This is a pure lyric, warm, exquisitely melodious, and sensuously beautiful, though somewhat sad. It is more difficult for young players than at first appears, in spite of its seeming simplicity, on account of the interlocking and occasionally interrupted figures of the accompaniment, but it is a fine study in sustained melody playing and dynamic balance of parts.

The mood is distinctly different from that in the well-known *Des Abends* by Schumann, although both deal with the quiet, dreamful, evening hour and are full of its subtle tenderness and veiled pathos. In this, the composer has evidently in mind a still, hazy evening in September, with its sense of vague depression, its faint floating odors of fading flowers and falling leaves, with the feeble breath of the dying summer just stirring the branches, and Nature's pulses perceptibly slowing down for the long winter's sleep. An hour when one half unconsciously sighs for the "might have been," recalling the fair blossoms of hope, now faded, and one's thoughts—like withered leaves—drift aimlessly on the sluggish current of memory. The closing measures are an unmistakable good-bye to the long, soft summer days.

Forest Elves. Schytté.

In notable contrast to the foregoing is the bright, playful, capricious *Wald Elfen*, full of sparkling fun and dainty tricksy roguery, a scherzo of the most perfect type. Here we have the elves at their midnight frolic in the cool, darksome glades of the forest, while a silver shower of moonbeams, falling through the leaves, works a shifting fairy patchwork on the mossy carpet and the "horns of Elfland, faintly blowing," mark the time for the steps of the mazy dance. This is a splendid study in combined lightness and accuracy, one of the most difficult achievements of piano-playing. It demands great speed, without apparent hurry; the utmost crispness and lightness of touch, united with certainty and flexibility. Above all, a perfect control of motor nerves and muscular mechanism. The player must *be* as the music should *sound*, intensely vitalized, keenly, joyously alive, yet perfectly cool. There must be no feverish flurry, no nervous slighting of notes, or fearsome stiffening of muscles. The apparent careless effervescence of hilarious spirits must be carefully studied and intelligently, though not apparently, controlled.

Berceuse (Cradle Song). Schytté.

One of the most melodically beautiful and charmingly winsome compositions by Schytté, or any composer since Chopin, is the *Berceuse*. With the exception of the inimitable and exquisite Chopin *Berceuse*, I regard this as far the best cradle song ever written for the piano.   It is perfect in form and detail.

The swaying rhythm of the accompaniment suggests throughout the rocking cradle, the soothing yet sensuous melody breathes the warmth and tenderness of maternal love, the peace and quiet of the summer twilight; while a certain rich glow and passionate fervor in the harmonic coloring stir the imagination, engendering the idea that the environment is tropical and Oriental, the scene some vine-wreathed villa in a rose garden of the far East, the singer perhaps a fair Georgian, whose flowing garments and loosened hair exhale the scent of myrrh and sandalwood, whose voice has caught the melting cadences from the tones of the nightingale, and whose dreams of the future of her child are woven of the fervid tints, the intoxicating perfumes, of the only world she knows.   Her song, like her emotions, is simple, but intense.

The utmost warmth and richness of tone quality is here demanded—full, deep, but velvet soft; a tone like the heart of a crimson rose.

Across the Steppes. Schytté.

This is a composition by Schytté which is comparatively little known, but is one of the most useful for
teaching purposes and one of the most original of his
smaller works, also a study in rapid, sustained wrist
movement and a fine recital number.

The Russian steppes are to our prairies what the
North Sea is to Lake Champlain,—vast, sombre, storm-
swept, enveloped much of the year in almost perpetual
darkness.

The rider must be imagined, not as a cow-boy, or a
sporting gentleman from New York, but as a Tartar
horseman, in the red and black uniform of the race.

The ride is a fast and furious gallop over the Russian
steppes, a dash for life into the frost-laden wind from
the Ural Mountains.

The rider is born to the saddle and seems a part of his
wild, half-broken steed, for he is a son of that race whose
ancestors, far back in the dim mythological past,
originated in the minds of the Greeks the legend of the
Centaur,—that fierce, fighting animal from the northern
wilds, half man, half horse, one and indivisible.

He rides at break-neck speed, savagely, sullenly, his
heart filled with a sombre fatalistic mood, as dark as the
night that closes in around him.

This work demands, and develops, a strong, supple
wrist. It must be given with an impetuous abandon
of style, much needed by certain pupils, and always
very effective with an audience.

Allegro from Sonata, Op. 53.   Schytté.

This is a much broader, more pretentious work than any thus far referred to.   In fact, it is a fully developed sonata of considerable magnitude, only to be handled successfully by advanced players.   For such, it will well repay careful study, especially the first movement. It is rich in musical content, and shows masterly skill in thematic development.   It has, moreover, a most interesting literary background.

It is founded on the old mythological epic of Finland, probably the oldest epic poem in existence, only recently translated into English, the *Kalevala*.   Incidentally it is worthy of note that the *Kalevala* is in form and rhythm identical in every particular with *Hiawatha*, and the claim has been made that the latter was a deliberate plagiarism on the part of Longfellow, but that is irrelevant here.

The allegro deals only with a part of the poem, namely, the Rune entitled *The Fate of Aino*.   She, according to the legend, was the sister of Youkahainen, the hero, poet and magician of Lapland.   He, in over-confidence, challenged to mortal combat, with the magic weapons of enchantment and incantation, the old and famous champion of Finland (also equipped as soldier, magician, and poet), and was completely overthrown and found himself sinking deeper and deeper in the freezing morass, under the relentless spells of his conqueror, till only his head remained in sight.

In vain he offered all his worldly goods for life and

relief, till in despair he bethought him of his sister, the lovely Aino, fairest of the Lapland maidens. Her he offers as bride to his tormentor, Wainamoinen, the old, grizzled, but formidable wizard of Finland, and the bride is accepted. Youkahainen is released and hastens home to make known his defeat, and prepare the sacrifice, while Wainamoinen follows more slowly, with pomp and splendor, to claim his bride. Aino, at his approach, terrified and despairing, flies to the white temple of the sea-god on a rock in the sea and prays to the god for protection. He, in answer, sends an earthquake, and the rock and the maiden sink to the bottom of the sea with crashing of thunder and mighty surging of billows:—

> "With a crash and roar of waters
> Falls the stone of many colors,
> Falls upon the very bottom
> Of the deep and boundless blue-sea,
> With the stone of rainbow colors
> Falls the weeping maiden Aino.
> Sleeping on the very bottom,
> In the caverns of the salmon,
> There to be the mermaid's sister,
> And the friend of nimble fishes."

This short quotation from the *Kalevala* gives the mood and the rhythm of the ancient poem, supposed to be more than three thousand years old.

The bold, pompous character of the opening theme of the sonata indicates the triumphant approach of the victorious bridegroom, his pride and power, and the tramp of the score of reindeers which draw his magnificent sleigh.

The plaintive second theme tells of the sorrow of Aino and her friends, and later of the united lament of the sea and forest; while the great ponderous climax portrays unmistakably the thunder crash of the catastrophe, which rescues, by destroying the heroine.

The story is not told consecutively in the music, or with definite sequence of events in detail, but the elements are all brought vividly before us.

The two remaining movements of the Sonata, *Intermezzo* and *Finale*, are musically inferior to the Allegro and are rarely played.

Nevin's Compositions.

The Narcissus. Nevin.

MONG Nevin's compositions for piano, the Narcissus undoubtedly stands first, on account of a certain rhythmic swing and easy flow of melody, which give it a semi-popular air, sometimes misleading to musicians in their estimate of its real merit. It has the direct unaffected sweetness and classic simplicity of a Greek pastoral, quite in harmony with the old familiar legend from which its name is derived.

In the golden days when myths were born of the first love between man's imagination and the charms of Nature, a youth of surpassing beauty, wandering by the side of a quiet stream, saw for the first time his own reflection in the mirror-like depths of the water. He supposed it to be the face of a water nymph, fell deeply in love with it, and lingered there day after day to watch and woo, until he died of love and longing.

From his grave upon the bank sprang the first Narcissus flower, named for him. Its pure delicate white and gold loveliness, its sweet seductive perfume, have insured it a place in the hearts of all races in all ages, as the symbol of a love stronger than life itself. A later Greek legend tells us that it was while gathering the narcissus or asphodel that Persephone, daughter of Ceres, was captured and borne away to the infernal regions to be the bride of Pluto. India and China revered the narcissus. The Egyptians placed wreaths of it about the embalmed dead, so that even now when a mummy is opened, a dried wreath of narcissus is sometimes found about its neck, the flowers of which bloomed more than two thousand years ago.

The Romans crowned their gods with garlands of narcissus and even the war-like Mohammed writes in the Koran: "He that has two cakes of bread, let him sell one of them for flowers of the narcissus: for bread is food for the body, but the narcissus is food for the soul."

In feudal days the narcissus stood for chivalry, as with the orientals in prehistoric ages it stood for immortality. The British corrupted the ancient name asphodel into Affodyle and then Daffodil, which designates today a certain type of narcissus in England and America.

Nevin, in his charming, sweet, simple little work, has embodied certainly the spiritual essence if not the actual story of the Greek myth, and it deserves a place in piano literature with Mendelssohn's Spring Song and Schumann's Träumerei, even though he was "only an American."

The Barcarolle. Nevin.

This composition, from the same set as the Narcissus, though by no means so widely known, deserves especial mention. It is a graceful, smoothly flowing, winsomely melodious work of no great difficulty, and is without doubt the best thing of its kind yet written by an American, not equalling, it is true, but closely approaching, in beauty, realistic effects and finished perfection, the famous Barcarolles by Rubinstein.

The Barcarolle, from *Barca*, a boat, is the Neapolitan boatman's song, with the rhythmic accompaniment of oars and murmur of the waves. The swing and splash of the oars, the rocking of the boat, the soft ripple of the placid water, are all deftly simulated in Nevin's composition; while the melody, though not so distinctively Italian in character as in Rubinstein's works of this type, is eminently suggestive. It depicts a calm, lovely moonlight scene on the blue Vesuvian bay, where happy lovers glide and dream, as if storm and disaster, whether on southern seas or in the emotional tides of the heart, were things unknown and impossible.

The Dragon Fly. Nevin.

Another exquisite little musical sketch from Nevin's hand is the Dragon Fly, a fantastic composition, full of sparkle and dainty witchery, suggesting the capricious flight of this erratic wanderer, flashing hither and thither, skimming the surface of a shallow stream, in pursuit of who knows what elfish sport or purpose.

The music is thoroughly representative in its playful vagaries, and as bright and rapid as the scintillations of swift iridescent wings. The piece is more difficult than the others mentioned, and requires a light crisp touch and easy, fluent technic. In this respect it is in the

9

same class with Grieg's Butterfly and Schumann's Bird as Prophet.

The Love Song. Nevin.

This little work for piano is invaluable as a study of tone production and phrasing.   It is one of Nevin's best lyrics, a love song in a broad, grave, manly vein, emotional, warm and impassioned, without becoming violent or hysterical.

It sings the love of a deep strong but well-poised nature, faithful and true but devoid of frenzy, like a fire that would warm and brighten a life, without consuming it.   It demands a quality of tone like that of the 'cello, deep, rich and resonant but never explosive.

In My Neighbor's Garden. Nevin.

This is one of Nevin's most fascinating and thankful compositions for the piano and but surprisingly little used.   It is constructed on the plan of the Chopin Impromptus, with a rapid sparkling first movement, and a slow pathetic minor trio or rather interlude, for it is hardly long enough to be properly designated as trio.

The opening movement is full of rustling leaves, fluttering wings, and silvery bird notes, the very breath of the spring garden and the jubilant ecstasy of mating birds.

In the interlude the mood changes suddenly to one of pensive depression and lonely longing.   Evidently there is something lacking in that spring, some presence missing in that garden.   The flowers and birds seem a sad mockery to the hungry heart.

But the sun shines on, the bright blossoms nod to the passing breeze, the bird's wild rapture continues, and the mood of Nature dominates the personal grief in a repetition of the first movement with some slight modifications; and the piece ends in a fountain-like spray of joyously ascending notes, like an irrepressible spring of gladness.

A facile dexterous finger technic is absolutely essential for this work, which is tricky and difficult, but must sound easy.

Miscellaneous Modern Compositions.

MID the mass of mostly insignificant compositions with which scores of would-be composers are flooding the market, there is occasionally one that stands forth with bold, commanding individuality like a giant among pigmies; compositions of real solid worth and originality, with something new and forceful to say for themselves as an excuse for being.

These exceptional products come, not from any one pen or nation, but seem to be sporadic growths in our overworked latter-day musical soil, where the all too abundant crop runs mostly to excessive leafage rather than to fruit. This is an age, not of genius but of generally diffused ability, of what Walt Whitman democratically extols as "divine averages," which means widespread but mediocre achievement, especially along all lines of artistic creation. The technic of composition, like that of piano playing, has become in a manner of speaking common property. Almost any one can write music, but few can write something worth writing, and they not always nor often.

The works referred to result from the specially stimulated efforts of exceptional men in exceptional moments. They mark the extreme high-water line of the rare flood-tides in such men's experiences, not their normal level. It is worthy of note, in view of the abuse which is lavished upon the taste and perception of the general public, how quickly and how almost universally such efforts are appreciated and such productions welcomed by the musical world.

Rachmaninoff. Prelude, Op. 3, No. 2.

This is one of the strongest productions of the new Russian school, Slavonic to its very marrow, original in every line, mighty with the untamed, uncompromising passions of a newly wakened, half-barbaric race, vital with the essence of a tremendous historic situation.

The scene is Moscow, the proud, the vanquished, in the midst of its illimitable snow-clad plains, in the first depressing gloom of the long winter night; its desolate streets resounding to the stern tread of Napoleon's victorious troops; Moscow, suddenly ablaze in every part, the torch applied by the hands of its fiercely sullen inhabitants; its costly palaces, its cosy homes, its vast accumulation of military stores consuming to ashes, and Napoleon's long cherished, all but fulfilled hope of safety and comfort for his vast army through the long winter, on which he has staked his all, going up in smoke before his eyes, and leaving four hundred thousand invading Frenchmen without food or shelter in the heart of a frozen desert; while the ponderous deep-throated bell of the Kremlin,

sounding the alarm, booms on above the rush and roar
of the flames, the crash of falling buildings, the shrieks
of the wounded, burned alive in the hospitals, and all
the confused terror and frenzy of destruction.

Through it all one feels the mingled triumph and
despair, the desperate, savage exultation of the Russian people, who have turned the foe's victory into
worse than defeat, by means of this fearful ally, the
all-devouring fire, and who glory, though with breaking hearts, in their own heroic sacrifice. It stirs the
depths of elemental passions slumbering in us all,
concealed by the pleasant observances and peaceful
seeming of our superficial civilization, as the treach-
erous slopes of Vesuvius have been covered by orchard
and vineyard and garden, till the eruption comes and
the lava stream pours its molten destruction over all.
In the closing chords one hears the slowly dying sigh
of spent fury, the hushed voice of uttermost darkness
and desolation.

D'Albert. Melodie.

D'Albert has given us a composition entitled "Melody," of intrinsic merit and originality almost equal
to the one just discussed, which however for some
reason has not as yet received the general recognition
it deserves, perhaps because of the very wild and unfamiliar mood which it expresses, and still more because
it deals apparently with purely abstract emotions in
their elemental simplicity, with no attempt to localize
them or give to them any special personification or
natural setting. In other words, it belongs to the class

of compositions known as emotional, not to that usually called descriptive.

That distinction is entirely erroneous, though so general that we are forced to recognize it, since music which expresses or portrays an emotion is just as descriptive in its way as that which delineates a scene in nature or in human life. In fact, strictly speaking, all music worthy of the name is descriptive. The difference lies merely in the character of the thing described.

Now while it is an undoubted fact that music is primarily the language of the emotions and always at its best when describing or expressing them, also that in most cases the introduction of the imitative element, such as the suggestion of storm or battle, tolling bells or rippling water, is intended only to supplement and intensify the emotional effect, still it is equally true that most persons, musicians as well as public, grasp and feel an emotion more fully and deeply if associated with some definite person in some particular situation, than if merely presented in an abstract form. For example, we sympathize with the love of Juliet more readily and more warmly than with love, the quality, put before us as an abstraction. So in music we are eager for any definite data bearing upon the personal origin or application of the moods we find expressed, and we welcome any realistic suggestions that will tend to localize the scene and connect the mood with some concrete human experience.

In cases where such definite data and realistic hints are wholly wanting, it is helpful and interesting to allow the imagination to find its own way back from

the general to the specific, from the mood expressed
to the probable or possible conditions which produced
it; to picture the approximate scene, setting and action
of which this mood is or might be the distilled essence.
The habit of such æsthetic analysis once formed is
a wonderful aid in the appreciation and interpretation
of every style of composition.

Let us try it with the work by D'Albert referred to,
with no guide but the internal evidence of the music
itself. Here we find one mood throughout, pronounced, sustained, unmistakable, a strong, dark, domi-
nating mood. It is a fierce yet gloomy courage, defying man and the elements, in the consciousness of
rugged, invincible strength and stern, inflexible deter-
mination; not courage that riots and exults under the
stimulus of action, the wild joy of battle, but courage
that sullenly, silently, bides its time, a waiting menace
to the foes it scorns yet longs to meet. The setting is
a background of midnight darkness through which is
felt the ominous threat of storm and the breath of an
icy cold. The only realistic suggestion is a hint of
rushing, foam-flecked waves in the agitated accompaniment.

Now suppose you were a painter and were called
upon to reproduce that mood and general impression
in a picture, by means of the representative symbolism
employed in that art. The mood must be personified in an actual man placed in a situation where it
would be appropriate and probable. That impression
of cold and darkness and agitation must be given by
a setting that includes those elements. What character and setting would you select for the purpose?

What scene so fitting as the North Sea, that synonym for darkness, storm, and mysterious terror? What character so suitable as that type of courage, strength, and endurance, and so appropriate in that setting, as the Norse Viking on his warship, daring the night and the gathering tempest on some reckless quest of spoil or vengeance, against a background of tumbling waves and black, wind-torn clouds?

You would paint a Danish war galley, lit by flaring torches, breasting the great seas with the foam flying from her cutwater, and in her prow the figure of the Viking fully armed, standing stern and motionless, but alert and watchful, instinct with intensest life, the embodiment of courage and confident power. And if you were a *great* painter you would make the beholder feel the danger, the bitter cold, the suppressed excitement and expectancy of the situation, as D'Albert makes us feel them in his music.

In the one case the scene is represented and the imagination supplies the resultant emotions. In the other the emotions are directly expressed and the imagination fills in the probable scene and causal conditions.

If you were a poet striving to produce the same impressions, you could neither express the emotion as directly as in music, nor present the scene as vividly as in painting, but would have to reach the imagination and the emotions through the intellect by means of the familiar symbolism of language. Your work would take the form of a story told in verse, describing the conditions and details as vividly as possible, enhanced by all the special resources of the poet's art at

your command. You might write something in this
vein:

> On the white-breasted billows
>   The good ship doth ride,
> And her decks are awash
>   With the spume of the tide.
> At the prow stands the Viking
>   In sea coat of leather,
> And laughs his disdain
>   In the teeth of the weather.
> How bitter the blast!
>   'Tis the iceberg's keen breath;
> And the surges are singing
>   Of danger and death.
> But with stern joy of combat
>   His nostrils dilate,
> As he stands, the embodied
>   Defiance of fate.
> With broadsword at belt,
>   And with axe burnished bright,
> He waits for the dawn
>   Through the storm and the night.
> With the swoop of the hawk
>   He'll descend on his prey;
> And his blade will drip blood
>   At the breaking of day.

If you are, unlike the writer, a *great* poet, the poem
would be much stronger, more finished and more complete, but the method employed would be the same, and
this will serve as illustration. To the present writer
nothing is more interesting or more illuminating than
to analyze and compare the laws underlying the different
arts and see how the same subject matter is treated
in the different forms, bearing always in mind that all
the arts are but different mediums of expression, and
that the soul of every art work is its content; the
peculiar beauty and fascination inherent in the material
and form of each special art should be of only secondary
importance. Too many artists are inclined to deify

the technic of their specialty, making that paramount, when in reality it is but a means to a much broader end, like the idiomatic charm of a dialect, which is only an adjunct, not a vital factor.

But to return to the D'Albert "Melody," shall we assume that it actually describes some such scene as I have outlined?   Not necessarily.   But it does express just such a mood as I have described, which might be accounted for or produced in the manner suggested.

Raff. Eclogue in G Flat.

This is a pure lyric, of about the fifth grade of difficulty, in the fluently melodious vein in which Raff was always at his best. The word eclogue was the Greek name of a certain type of pastoral poem, a short, simple poem in a tranquil, tender mood, describing rural scenes in which shepherds appeared, singing and playing upon the flute. Raff has cleverly utilized the name and the idea in connection with several short compositions for the piano, of which this is perhaps the best.

The mood suggested by his chosen Greek model in verse has been admirably expressed by the composer in this music.   It is soft, gentle, and pensive, but without sadness or more intense moments to break its restful placidity. It possesses, too, a pronounced pastoral character, even on casual examination.

The imagination of the listener readily supplies the rustic scene as a fitting background for the tone-picture, a sunlit mountain slope, its green expanses dotted with grazing sheep, which have been, since time began, the symbols of rural peace and plenty; in the shadow of a little grove a party of shepherds resting, watching their flocks and whiling away the long hours of the summer afternoon with simple music of their own making. One sings a simple, tender song—a love song, it may be—to the quiet accompaniment of the guitar or zither. Another contributes a delicate flute obligato, the light notes falling in a crystal shower above and around the sustained tones of the melody, like dewdrops shaken from wind-tossed branches.

The song-like theme in the right hand suggests the voice of the shepherd. It should be given with a firm, clinging pressure touch. It should sound full, but not loud, and be well sustained, perfectly legato, and very clearly phrased. This phrasing must be maintained with equal distinctness at the repetition, when the flute-like obligato is added, so that it may be easily followed. The quiet arpeggio accompaniment in the left hand must be subdued, of course, to a mere harmonious murmur, producing as nearly as possible the illusion of the effect of harp or guitar.

The flute runs in the upper register should be light as a breath, yet clear as crystal, so as to embellish, without in the least obscuring, the melody. It should be demi-staccato, played with the very tips of well-curved fingers. The piece affords opportunities for study in relative dynamic effects and various tone-qualities, and is a grateful number for the player.

The Night has a Thousand Eyes, by Ferdinand Dewey.

"The night has a thousand eyes,
    The day but one;
But the light of the whole world dies
    With the dying sun.

The mind has a thousand eyes,
    The heart but one;
But the light of the whole life dies
    When love is done."

The beauty, tenderness, and pathos of these brief lines are reproduced in the music with a fidelity and finish worthy of a Chopin.   In fact, though written by a comparatively obscure American musician, whose place in the hearts of his sorrowing friends is far larger and more justly awarded than in the temple of fame, this composition has few equals in its line from any pen in any land.

The melody, considered with or without the words, is a song of the heart, as simple, as concise, and as universally appealing as the thought in the lines which inspired it.   It is another fine study in tone-quality and inflection.

The accompaniment, though admirably written, enhancing and enriching the effect of the melody, if well rendered, offers a problem in left-hand technic not too easily solved even by the professional artist. The figures are involved and unusual, a tax of no common order on the memory as well as the finger dexterity, and for that very reason furnish an excellent left-hand study, well up in the sixth grade.   These sinuous, interwoven runs, with their subtle, chromatic modulations and their shadowy suggestions of half-veiled bits of counterpoint, produce a dreamy, elusive effect, a veritable *chiaro-oscuro* of sound, reminding one of the soft, starry summer night and of Tennyson's lines in reference to the Pleiades:

> "Like a swarm of golden fire-flies
> Tangled in a silver braid."

The Dryad, by Jensen.

The Dryad is one of a charming set of Idyls for the Piano, by Jensen, a modern German writer of the romantic school, with no great profundity and no startling originality of conceptions, but with a genial, fluent and often remarkably clever manner of expression, and a delicate, refined fancy which should commend him to a more general recognition than he seems at present to enjoy.   In the midst of the fervid intensity of most modern music, Jensen's work is occasionally as refreshing and restful as the pearl grey tints and fern-scented coolness of some rock-shadowed grotto in the heart of a sun-flooded, tropical rose-garden.   This composition, in form a song without words, in that most optimistic of keys—G major—has a breezy freshness, a natural, simple grace which characteristically express the personality it is intended to suggest.

The Dryad, a Greek nymph of the forest, one of Pan's court and one of the most unsophisticated and simple of all those joyous children of nature, was a personification of the life of the tree, its vital principle or soul.   From a realistic standpoint we may fancy this to be the Dryad's song, a little vesper hymn of praise to the setting sun, sung in quiet, happy confidence to the accompaniment of the murmuring leaves above her head. This whispering, murmurous effect, as of leaves and branches stirred by the evening breezes, is given in the left hand continuously throughout the piece, and should receive special attention from the player with this idea in mind. The rapidity and delicacy of the left-hand passages, with their proper shading, constitute the chief difficulty of the work. The soprano melody, carried by the right hand, may be supposed to typify the Dryad's voice, full of her own fresh, child-like individuality. The mood of the whole work is eminently characteristic and replete with woodland witcheries.

Dance of the Elves, Sapellnikoff.

The "Dance of the Elves," by Sapellnikoff, one of the most gifted and promising of the many Russian composers of the day, himself a concert pianist of growing fame, a pupil and protégé of Mme. Sophia Menter, is one of his brightest and most popular works, frequently appearing on his own concert programs. The conception of the character and attributes of the Elf varies widely in the mythologies of different lands and races. The English Elf, for instance, is a merry, harmless, though roguish little dweller of the green-wood, almost as dainty and winsome as the fairy, but given to droll humor and tricky pranks. The German Elf, especially as found in the depths of the Black Forest, is a far more fearsome apparition, of much greater stature and power and more intense and sinister personality. Notably the Elf King, who figures in so many weird German ballads, is a potent and vindictive monarch of the gloomy solitudes, wielding the power of life and death over mortals, while his Queen is a most beautiful, but wicked, siren-like being, dangerous to the souls as well as the bodies of men. In Russia again the Elf is the gleesome, frolicsome child of this North land and the Winter, the embodied spirit of the swift, sparkling hail shower and the flying snow-flakes. It is he who piles the drifts in such fantastical shape; who traces those wondrous pictures on the frosted window-pane; who festoons the drooping pines with countless ice crystals, which glitter like prisms in the light and tingle like fairy sleigh-bells when swung by the laughing North wind. This composition pictures a dance by these blythe little snow-sprites. The time is a winter night, the place a moon-lit forest glade. The setting of the scene is unbroken white; the dance floor, the level-frozen snow. Ice-covered trees—like knights in silver armor—stand as stately chivalrous spectators of the festival. In the centre of the dancers the Elf Queen stands, and once in the midst of the dance she brings all to a stand and holds their attention for a moment while she makes what seems to be a little address of welcome, it may be, or of warning, or narrates some legend of Elf-land, after which the dance is resumed with increased vivacity. The music graphically portrays not only the mood and movement of the dance, with all its spirit and sparkle, but the whole frost-embroidered scene—cold, crisp, dazzling. It is one of those singular transmutations, sometimes found in Art, where the impressions, usually obtained through

one sense, are carried over into the realm commonly
appertaining to another; where, for instance, effects
generally recognized only by the eyes are made, to
some extent, perceptible to the ear, as in this case, where
the result might almost be called audible frost-work.

Rustle of Spring, by Ch. Sinding.

It is a recognized fact that all composers, not less
than authors, are materially influenced in temperament,
habit of thought, general style and choice of subject,
by their geographical and climatic surroundings, as well
as by their racial heredity.

This is especially true of the Scandinavian composers,
probably because of the strikingly prominent and individual characteristics of their native land, with its
rugged, yet fascinating scenery, its wild rock-ribbed,
snow-covered mountains, its smiling valleys, its sombre
pine forests, its flashing, tumbling streams, and its
broken irregular coast line, white with the flying foam
of restless breakers, its sharp contrasts of frozen winter
midnight and fervid, glowing, summer days—all of
which cannot fail of their effect on the imagination.

Such environment and conditions have helped to give
to the ancient mythology and to the more recent art
products of the Northland their peculiarly original
stamp.   They are, in part at least, responsible for the
unusual type of genius of such men as Ibsen, Björnson,
Grieg and Sinding.

In these Northern latitudes the spring comes swiftly,
suddenly, with an impetuous rush.   The ardent blus-
tering south-wind sweeps triumphantly over the icy
10

battlements of the frost-king's defences, breaking, at
a touch, the fetters of the mountain torrents, waking
the flowers from their long winter sleep and arousing
nature, with his jubilant voice, to prepare for her
bridal with the coming Spring. This ever-recurring
phenomenon, in past centuries, gave rise to the beautiful allegorical legend of the Sleeping Beauty, that
enchanted lady in the dread castle of sleep, guarded
by her stern jailor, representing the Northland in its
winter trance under the spell of Jack Frost, while her
rescuing lover, the Fairy Prince, who wakes her with
a kiss to life and love, was the spring. His impatient approach, accompanied by rushing winds and
rustling leaves, the ripple of glad waters and the murmur of welcoming forests, is represented in this composition, which is justly one of the most popular of recent
works for the piano. It literally imitates the gusty
rush of spring-winds, the chatter of wayward brooks,
the all-pervading stir and rustle and murmur, which tell
of the quickening of new life throughout all nature, the
thrilling of her pulses at the revivifying kiss of spring;
while the warm emotional character of the melody and
the rich, sensuous harmonies, with their constantly
recurring sevenths and ninths and frequent suspensions,
suggest the vague, half mystical, half passionate longings, the indefinable unrest, the subtle blending of joy
and sadness, which wake and stir and swell and surge in
the human heart at the voice of spring.

The Wedding Day, by Grieg.

This composition, in Grieg's most characteristic vein, was written for the anniversary celebration of his own wedding day, which took place at his country home among the mountains, fantastically named Troldhaugen, which means home or stronghold of the Trolls—the *Gnomes* of the Norseland. The composition is in the march form, with strongly marked rhythms, weird, suggestive harmonies and simple, but original melodies. It simulates the music at an old-time, rustic festival among the rugged, robustly hilarious northern races— rough as their mountains, wild as their tempestuous seas, boisterous as their winter winds, yet wholesome, kindly and given to harmless, if rather rude, merry- making. The spirit of frolic is not lost in the land of the midnight sun.

Grieg, who was a typical Norseman at heart, was deeply interested in all the ancient myths, traditions and customs of his country, and these intimate home- festivals at his country-seat on his wedding anniversary were arranged in keeping with the spirit and habit of the olden days, including a revival of the old rude games, trials of strength and various classically antique forms of amusement of the rural sort.

In this music Grieg has not only expressed the prim- itive, whole-hearted gayety and fantastic pranks of the festival, but has introduced several realistic suggestions to heighten the illusion and maintain the artistic verities of the tone picture, as, for example, the sound of drum and fife recurrent and unmistakable, and the peculiar droning bass and whining melody characteristic of the bagpipe, that most distinctly rustic instrument.

By the way, it is a mistake to identify the bagpipe exclusively with the Scottish clans and their music. True, the Scots used the bagpipe in war and peace as their favorite, and almost their only instrument of camp and field, as the harp was that of the ladies' bower, but the "ancient and honorable" bagpipe, in some of its many modifications and under different names, was familiarly used by all the Teutonic races, including the Scandinavians, and, to some extent, by the Latins, especially in southern Italy and islands of the Mediterranean. Hence the monotonous drone of the bagpipe, simulated in constantly reiterated fifths in the bass, as an accompaniment for country dances of all lands, is common and legitimate.

The central idea of this wedding day music is the march of the assembled guests to the place of meeting, where a plentiful rustic feast is spread under the trees and where the games are to take place, the music growing louder and more spirited and impetuous as they approach their destination, ending in an excited burst of rollicking hilarity as some of the more lusty youths break rank and join in a mad race for the goal.

Before this final clamorous outburst, however, there is a curious little interlude, a quaint bit of rather stilted lyric in "canon" form, where the voices follow and answer each other as if in a dialogue. It is a brief touch of sentiment, old-fashioned in its expression, but genuine. A hint of a stolen exchange of warmer looks and words between the bride and groom,—a moment in which they forget the festive scene and noisy company, engrossed with their own old yet eternally new love story.

Doumka, by Tschaikowsky.

As a piano composer Tschaikowsky is, comparatively speaking, "an unknown quantity" to the majority of American music teachers, partly because of the weirdly fantastic, ultra Russian character of his pianoforte works, which are not very numerous, partly because, according to his own admission, they are not strictly what the Germans call "clavier-mässig," that is, adapted to the piano. Yet there are some among them, which, in spite of this strong foreign flavor and his naïve disregard of pianistic limitations, are strikingly interesting and in the modern frantic scramble for novelties it is a wonder that they are so largely neglected. To this class belongs "Doumka," a *thought*. It is descriptive only in the strictly symbolic sense, expressing grave, in fact, deeply gloomy reflection and the profound, intensely melancholy emotions arising from it.

It is a thought, or rather a series of thoughts, concerned with that most serious and solemn, as well as most painful of all subjects with which the human mind can grapple, the ultimate finality, death. In addition to the vast significance, the vague terrors, the awesome majesty of the subject in the abstract, it introduces, and dwells upon, the more specific idea and more personal mood of a rustic funeral scene, in all its sorrowful details.

The principal theme, slow, impressive, intense, mournful, in its constant monotonous reiteration, rep-

resents the death song, or chant, of the mourners, generally in use among all races from the early Greeks—
and probably long prior to their time—up to a comparatively recent epoch, and still in vogue in the rural
districts of Russia, a sort of dirge sung sometimes by
the friends of the deceased, sometimes by professional
mourners, specially trained for that purpose, but always
expressing the mood of the time and the occasion,
now tearfully plaintive, now passionately despairing,
but suggesting always by its persistent iteration the
endless hopelessness of the dread event.

The steady, solemn march of the procession is indicated throughout the composition, symbolically significant of the relentless tread of that inexorable *fate*
which plays so important a part in the beliefs and conceptions of the Sclaves. The work closes with a
sudden, startling crash of heavy harmonies like the
clanging to of the door of a tomb—harsh, metallic, as
it shuts forever upon hope and effort, joy and love.

The scene is autumn, cold and brown and bare, with
no hint of promise, no touch of color anywhere. The
mood is the blackest that can be expressed in music, a
mighty tragedy in tone.

Troika en Traineaux, by Tschaikowsky.

This, odd, jolly, half-facetious bit of descriptive
writing for the pianoforte shows us the composer in a
light, playful mood very unusual with him, and it
forms the strongest possible contrast to the work just
described.

The *troika* is a Russian vehicle used in the rural districts.   It has two wheels, a rude open body and no springs.   It is usually harnessed with three horses abreast, the middle one wearing a string of bells similar to our sleigh bells.   They are generally driven at a furious gallop over the interminable stretches of rough country road, with much shouting and cracking of the cruel whip, the drivers sparing neither themselves nor their teams, the bells marking their pace with wild clangor and clash.

In winter the wheels are removed from the troika and the body is fastened upon a sort of sledge, making a kind of sleigh or *traineau*.   Hence the title "Troika en Traineaux," meaning in its winter guise.

In this music the melody simulates a Russian folk-song, simple, catching, rollicking; supposed to be sung by the Russian peasant driver, much in the mood of Schumann's *Happy Farmer*, while the horses swing along at a lively pace and the cumbersome troika, on its rude runners, rocks and bumps and slues down the icy, rutty road, the driver evidently in haste to reach the place of some rustic merry making and jovially hilarious in anticipation of the frolic to come.

In the latter part the sound of the merry bells is distinctly imitated.   The whole thing is a musical jest, full of the rough, simple jollity of the Russian peasant on one of his rare holidays, and remarkable, in all its simplicity, for its strong local flavor.

Cracovienne, by Paderewski.

This is a sparkling, spirited and eminently characteristic composition, of moderate difficulty and great musical charm; one of the best of Paderewski's smaller works, indeed, fully equal in merit to his famous Menuet though not nearly so well known.

The Cracovienne, or Krakoviak as it is interchangeably called, was originally a rude, wildly impetuous, rustic dance among the peasants of Cracow, formerly a large and important province of Poland of which Cracow was the capital, also at one time the capital of all Poland.

In the good old primitive days, when men had less, knew less and enjoyed more than at present, when the ruddy rollicking autumn in russet coat and scarlet wreath came stalking jovially down from the north over the plains of central Europe, bringing to the lusty peasant rest and good cheer after the summer's work in the fields, and leisure for all sorts of merry-making; when the grain had been harvested and stored, and the dull thunder of the flails was stilled, then came the time for the great autumn festival, similar to the "harvest-home" of old England and the still earlier "Herbst-fest" of the Teutons.

Some barn of amplest proportions was selected as the *rendezvous*, the great threshing-floor was cleared and swept, the rude walls festooned with garlands of bright leaves, and the peasants from far and near assembled for the festive celebration, the chief feature of which was the dancing of the Cracovienne. This function combined with all the exciting fascination of the usual rough country dance, a peculiar, purely local element all its own, "The strife of torches." Around the walls (commonly of unhewn stone and plaster) were fastened at regular intervals, several feet from the floor, a large number of flaming torches. In the course of the dance each couple took its turn in passing around the entire hall next the wall immediately beneath this row of lights. The man who could extinguish, with his foot, the greatest number of torches (a single high kick being allowed for each), without missing his step in the dance, disconcerting his partner, or losing his balance and sprawling on the floor, was the champion of the evening, and was awarded as a prize a dance and a kiss by any girl he might choose as the prettiest in the assembly.

Naturally, the frantic attempts of the various swains to excel each other, in this rather strenuous feat, and their frequent failures and ludicrous mishaps, were provocative of the greatest excitement and the most noisy hilarity, and it is highly probable that in the darkness following the fall of the last torch, many a kiss was taken not strictly in accordance with the rules of the game.

The Cracovienne, like most ancient dances, has furnished the vital germ for a modern musical art form, elaborated and idealized, but conforming in general character to the original mood and movement, including the most essential features, as in this instance, for example, the sudden comical effect of the *high kick* to be found in every good Cracovienne.

The work by Paderewski referred to is a fine specimen of its class, a thought too much idealized, perhaps a fraction too dainty and refined; for the rough peasant appears here to have donned an evening suit, with clean collar and cuffs. The atmosphere is rather that of the perfumed, modern ball-room than the dust and chaff-laden air of the old granary; but the *verve* and zest and humor are all retained in large measure. The music is piquant, brilliant and playful, full of odd rhythmic devices and fascinating melodies, and the droll suggestions of the *high kicking* are frequent and unmistakable.

Baba Yaga, Capriccioso by LeRoy B. Campbell

This original and wildly fantastic composition in A minor, by L. B. Campbell (one of our rising American writers) will be found to be an interesting and welcome novelty, either as a concert number or for use with advanced pupils. It is founded upon an old weird Russian legend, and Mr. Campbell's recent sojourn in Russia and his familiarity with its legendary lore, as well as with the modern style and peculiar atmosphere of Russian music, eminently fit him to give appropriate expression to the subject in tone.

Baba Yaga was the oldest, wildest and wickedest, as well as the most potent of all the Russian witchwives, the leader of the band. She dwelt alone, in a rude hut on the shore of a black, storm-swept lake, in the depths of a sombre ghoul-haunted forest.

Here, amid the drifting acrid smoke of the fire, and the noxious vapors from the great witch-cauldron, she brewed her deadly poisons, muttered her gruesome incantations and danced her frantic spell-working dances; and here any who sought her aid in working secret mischief to a foe, must brave the terrors of the woods at dead of night and seek her.

The music is intended to represent the wild sinister mood of the scene, the frenzied delirium of the dance, and even from time to time the blood-curdling shrieks of the dancer.

It should be given with the utmost fire and dash, with a hard, dry quality of tone like the rattle of bones, or wooden castanets, and with a certain rough angularity of outline, indicating the rude, primitive character of the scene being enacted and the personages taking part in it.

Nocturne, by J. M. Blose.

As elsewhere stated in these pages, in connection with Schumann's Nachtstück, the Nocturne is a night-piece, properly embodying nocturnal scenes, moods, and experiences, and including within its possible and legitimate scope a wide range and variety of subjects and emotions, but all associated with the night in its manifold aspects.

This Nocturne by Blose, though written by an American, is a fine specimen of its class, clear and symmetrical in form, broad and forceful in style, rich in varied and original harmonic coloring and scholarly in thematic development.

It is no lover's dream of a summer eve, soft and sweet and tender, but a strong, bold sketch of an autumn night, in all its sombre majesty; a night of gloom and sudden storm, of flying clouds and gusty rain, with moments of hushed suspense, ominous of tragedy, broken by bursts of tempestuous, elemental passion; the fitting symbol and setting for a strong man's sorrow and conflict, and desperate, but courageous wrestlings with the powers of darkness within and without.

The mood is gloomily heroic, suggesting at times the most dominant element in Scandinavian music.

The work is in a sense allegorical, for I know, from personal acquaintance with the writer, that the night portrayed was that of the spirit, during a transient experience of grief and struggle, rather than of nature; and the tempest one of emotion, not of the elements. The music is doubly interesting for this dual significance.

The brief but beautiful Trio, in the tender lyric vein, affords the requisite reposeful contrast, suggesting a glint of moon-light through the rifted clouds, a touch of rest and peace and brightness in the midst of darkness and turmoil, a gleam of the white wings of hope across the stormy sea of emotion.

Then the first subject returns and night and tempest again dominate the scene for a time; but the gravely quiet finale seems to give promise of a tranquil dawn.

I have ventured to include here a few of my own descriptive compositions which have been most successful in concert work and about which I have received many inquiries.   The first four are not too difficult for sixth grade pupils, but the last one is only possible for very advanced players.

Die Lorelei, by Edward Baxter Perry.

DIE LORELEI.

After the German of Heine.

1.

The air grows cool and it darkens,
And tranquilly flows the Rhine;
And kissed by the glow of sunset
The peaks of the mountains shine.

2.

High o'er the gliding river,
A maiden, wondrous fair,
Sits in the golden twilight,
And combs her golden hair.

3.

With a golden comb she combs it,
And sings a song the while,
With a wild and witching melody,
The listener to beguile.

4.

It reaches the ear of the boatman,
On the river's breast below,
And quickens his heart to a passion
Of love and longing and woe.

5.

Erect in his fragile vessel,
He stands spellbound by its might;
He sees not the rocks and the rapids,
He gazes alone on the height.

6.

Engulfed by the angry billows,
The boatman sinks anon:
And this with her siren singing,
The Lorelei hath done.

This composition, like all other "Loreleis," is descriptive, and based upon the most famous of the Rhine legends, that of the Lorelei Siren. The fantasy was conceived by the writer when approaching and passing by boat the Lorelei rocks on the Rhine, a mass of bare black boulders, rising abruptly from the water to a height of about 150 feet, at whose base runs the most dangerous set of rapids on the river, and on whose summit the Lorelei Siren was supposed to perch and sing at twilight, to the intoxication and destruction of the boatmen below, who, spellbound by the witchery of her voice and face, forgot to keep midway in the current, and perished on the rocks at her feet.

The composition is supposed to open at some little distance from the Lorelei rock, with a tranquil running accompaniment in the left hand, indicating the twilight flow of the river, with a broken thread of melody, which occasionally wells to the surface in a single detached note, suggested by that line of Tennyson's "With an inner voice the river ran." As we draw nearer the scene of the legend, we catch snatches of the silver laughter of the Siren, mingled with the distant ripple of the water, at the foot of the famous rock. Then rises clearly the Lorelei's song, sweet and vibrant, but neither passionate nor powerful, alluring rather than compelling, with the running accompaniment of the water ever present. This mood is held throughout the first recital of the entire melody, but with a slight increase of strength, a little fuller pulsation, as we are supposed to approach. At its sudden cessation is heard the boatman's song, a minor theme in strong contrast, suggestive of the mood and character of the boatman on the river below, of the "love and longing and woe" which "quicken his heart" at sight of the siren and sound of her song. This sinister theme, with its turbu-

lent accompaniment, grows in intensity and passion to a
vehement climax, which indicates the catastrophe of
the legend, the engulfing of boat and boatman at the
foot of the Lorelei rock. It is followed by a few incoherent phrases of no melodic form, swirls of the gurgling
water where it has opened, diminishing rapidly to
pianissimo, when the Lorelei's song again arises, this
time jubilant and strong, ringing out over the river,
above the roar of the rapids, as she gloats over her
victim, and working up to a second climax of vindictive
glee. This subsides as we are supposed to leave the
rock behind us, till we hear only broken fragments of
the melody and snatches of laughter in the distance as
before; and finally, nothing is left but the peaceful
theme in the left hand which formed the introduction
of the composition, the tranquil flow of the river, with
the "inner voice."

Aeolienne. Edw. Baxter Perry.

"But once they set
A stringed gourd on the sill, there where the wind
Could linger o'er its notes and play at will—
Wild music makes the wind on silver strings—
And those who lay around heard only that;
But Prince Siddartha heard the Devas play,
And to his ears they sang such words as these:

"We are the voices of the wandering wind,
Which moan for rest and rest can never find;
Lo! as the wind is, so is mortal life,
A moan, a sigh, a sob, a storm, a strife.

"Wherefore and whence we are ye cannot know,
Nor where life springs nor whither life doth go;
We are as ye are, ghosts from the inane,
What pleasure have we of our changeful pain?

"What pleasure hast thou of thy changeless bliss?
Nay, if love lasted, there were joy in this;
But life's way is the wind's way, all these things
Are but brief voices breathed on shifting strings."
                    —*From Edwin Arnold's Light of Asia.*

This composition was suggested by the above lines, the sentiment of which I have attempted to express through an imitation of Aeolian harp effects, as literal as the limitations of the pianoforte and the necessities of musical construction would permit. The player should endeavor firstly to reproduce, as realistically as possible, the soft, plaintive, mysterious murmur of wind-swept strings; and secondly, by means of tone effects and melodic shading, to suggest to the listener the thoughts and moods embodied in the poet's lines.

The Portent. Edw. Baxter Perry.

This composition was suggested by George Mc-Donald's romance of the same name, or rather by the ancient and uncanny Scotch legend about which the plot of his story is ingeniously woven.

As the result of a peculiarly grewsome tragedy in the history of one of the Highland clans, whose chief, on account of his horse's loose and broken shoe, was hurled over the edge of a precipice while riding at full galop, with the unconscious form of his cousin and lady-love over his saddle bow, the descendants of this family for many generations became the victims of a strange and singular hallucination, taking sometimes the form of that second sight so familiar in Scotch folk-lore, sometimes a sort of second hearing, a phenom-

enal acuteness of ear, which forced them to perceive
now sights, now sounds from the spectral world, to
which all others were oblivious.   One manifestation in
particular was most frequent and came to be dreaded
as the family Portent.   Every important catastrophe
occurring to any member of this family was heralded
by the sound, at first distant, then swiftly approaching,
then deafening, of a fiercely galoping horse with a loose
and clanking shoe.

It is this audible Portent that I have endeavored to
embody in the following work, beginning faint and
distant, suspected rather than heard, a fear rather than
a sound, rapidly growing, however, till the rhythmic
swing of the horse's galop is distinctly audible, crossed
now and then by the sinister clank of the broken shoe.

After the first impetuous climax, a plaintive interlude is intended to suggest the moment when second
sight asserts itself, in a passing spectral glimpse of a wild
horseman, a jet-black steed, and the fair pale face of the
maiden, lying across the saddle, her long dark hair
streaming in the wind.   This vision vanishes and the
horse's galop is heard faster and fiercer than before,
rising rapidly to the final climax, when he passes in
immediate proximity, then as rapidly diminishing,
fading, dying into distance and silence.

Autumn Reverie. Edw. Baxter Perry.

This composition is not objectively descriptive,
but is a mood picture, aiming to embody the emotions,
half sad, half passionately rebellious, of a strong but
sensitive soul struggling with the depressing influences

of a sullen autumnal evening, in which it traces a
sympathetic reflection of its own moods. Falling
leaves and fading flowers, the fitful moaning of the
wind and the grey cloud-canopy veiling the sky, sym-
bolize fleeting joys, false promises, vain endeavor, and
vanishing hope, the futility of effort, however courageous, and the certainty of sorrow, however ill-deserved.
The following lines are the expression of the same mood
in verse:

> "All my roses are dead in my garden—
>   What shall I do?
> Winds in the night, without pity or pardon,
>   Came there and slew.

> "All my song-birds are dead in their bushes—
>   Woe for such things!
> Robins and linnets and blackbirds and thrushes,
>   Dead, with stiff wings.

> "What shall I do for my roses' sweetness,
>   The summer round,—
> For all my garden's divine completeness
>   Of scent and sound?

> "I will leave my garden for winds to harry;
>   Where once was peace,
> Let the bramble-vine and the wild brier marry,
>   And greatly increase.

> "But I will go to a land men know not,—
>   A far, still land,
> Where no birds come, and where roses blow not,
>   And no trees stand."
>   —*Philip Bourke Marston*

Ballade of Last Island.
Edw. Baxter Perry.

In *Harper's Magazine* for April, 1888, appeared a remarkably graphic sketch by Lafcadio Hearn, entitled
"Chita; or, A Memory of Last Island: The Legend of
L'Ile Dernière." It dealt with the destruction of Last
Island, formerly a fashionable watering-place in the
Gulf of Mexico, thronged every season with hundreds of
aristocratic guests from the Southern States. On the
10th of August, 1856, at the height of the season, the
island was totally destroyed by a sudden tempest and
tidal wave. Every vestige of human habitation was
swept into the Gulf and nearly every soul of the hundreds there assembled perished.

The composition is a musical transcript, almost
page for page, of Mr. Hearn's perfect and powerful
prose poem. It opens with a quiet lyric introduction,
intended to portray the mood of the bland, ethereal
azure days preceding the storm, which the author describes as "Days born in rose and buried in gold, when
winds held their breath and slow wavelets caressed the
bland brown beach with a sound as of kisses and whispers, and for weeks no fleck of cloud broke the heaven's
blue dream of eternity." Then the first mighty pre-
monitory rollers come surging in from the far horizon,
to break slowly in whispered thunder upon the strand,
indicated in the composition by a few sweeping, wave-
like arpeggios. The principal theme of the work, which
follows, portrays the rising, ominous voice of the sea,

which, to quote Mr. Hearn again, "Is not one voice, but a tumult of many voices, voices of drowned men, the muttering of the multitudinous dead, all rising to rage against the living at the great witch-call of storms."

Steadily the gale increases, the gloom deepens, and the surf breaks higher, till toward midnight, when the storm has nearly reached its climax, there is a sudden lull, and winds and waves are hushed in suspense. In this moment of tranquillity, merry, mocking strains of waltz music are heard drifting out upon the gloom and terror of that tempestuous night from the ball-room of the great summer hotel upon the island.

Just here I have introduced a waltz of a light, almost flippant character, in contrast to the sombre themes and harmonies which precede and follow, suggesting the mood as well as the movement of the dancers.

The incongruous strains reach the ear of the veteran captain of the steamer Morning Star, which, dragging three anchors, is drifting down to her inevitable doom amid the breakers, and he exclaims, "Dancing! God help them! for the wind dances with the sea to-night, and if he takes a notion to whip around south, there'll be dancing to a different tune!" In the repetition and development of the waltz-theme, I have endeavored to depict the moment when the wind veers and "from the south he comes on, with the strength of a tornado and the sound of a cannonade, bearing the sea, a blanched and frightened partner, in his arms, and the very land trembles to this giant tread, as but a moment since the polished floor of the dance hall quivered to the pressure of circling steps."

Then the original sea-theme returns, with its sobbing,

surging accompaniment, the voice of the sea again, but rising to a shout of warning, and the tempest rapidly increases to the final climax and ultimate awful catastrophe, when "Shattered wrecks of buildings, mingled with uprooted trees and struggling human victims, are swept surging together, in a weltering chaos of destruction, out into the black waters of the Gulf." Then, like the storm, the composition gradually subsides in sad, falling cadences, like repentant surges sobbing themselves to rest on a wreck-strewn shore; and at the close are a few subdued minor chords, a musical requiescat for the lost.

Musicians will notice that the theme of the Coda is identical with that of the introduction, only given in extension and in the minor key, to suggest that it is the same scene, the same sea and sky, but altered almost beyond recognition by the passing of the shadow of Death.

Teaching Pieces for Second and Third Grades.

SCARCELY a week passes that I do not receive requests for a list of pieces in these earlier grades that are at once meritorious and pleasing, well made and practically usable. My personal experience with music of this grade is very limited, but I will mention a few such compositions which have come to my notice and which I know to be available and useful of their kind. Some of them may be new to the reader.

First let me say that in the study of the piano, as in other lines, every stage has its mental as well as its technical limitations, which the good teacher must recognize.

It is as unwise to insist on an exclusive diet of the classics for the young, undeveloped pupil, as to feed a baby on roast-beef and mince-pie; or to force a child in the primary school to read only Browning and Emerson. The effect is as certain to be detrimental.

Bohm, Spindler, and even Lange are better musical nourishment for the child than Schumann or Bach; for the taste as well as technic must grow gradually and nutrition must be adapted to the digestive capacity of the recipient.

There are many small compositions, good, yet attractive to the young student, and well suited to meet the need in question.   Among American writers who have supplied much valuable material of this class none ranks higher than my old friend, the lamented Fred L. Morey, formerly of Chicago.

His works will prove a treasure-trove to those not familiar with them.

They are melodious, easily grasped, and free from technical complexities.

Gavotte Imperial in A minor, by Morey.

Here is a fine study in octave and chord work, invaluable to the student in the first stage of development in that line.   Musically it is strong, stirring, and martial in character, with a fine melodious Trio, and is an excellent specimen of that form of dance music. For full description of the Gavotte see the "Story of the Gavotte" in this volume.

Among the same set of six pieces, is a fine Cradle-song in G.

Song of the Kankakee, by Morey.

This is a useful and attractive study in rippling arpeggio figures, with a sustained tuneful melody in the middle register.   It is well made, both musically and technically, is interesting and practicable for the pupil, and, as it is but little known, will prove a welcome novelty to teachers who are looking for good yet pleasing third-grade pieces.

It is a musical memory of Mr. Morey's boyhood, many of its happiest hours having been spent on the willow-fringed banks of the tranquil Kankakee, watching the changing lights and shadows on the surface of the dimpling water, listening to the low, slumberous murmur of the languid stream as it wound its slow way through the fertile plains of Illinois, while he lay in the shadow, among the whispering willows and alders, and dreamed a boy's dreams of the days to come, when he should be a great composer and write mighty symphonies for the world's orchestras to perform, while listening thousands rejoiced and applauded— dreams which, like most of those of youth, were destined to remain unfulfilled.

Poor Morey! He died, like Spindler and Heller and Schubert and Mozart, and a score of other greater men than he, in obscurity and poverty; but a few of us remember him loyally as the best of friends, a prince of good fellows, and a musician gifted far beyond the lot of most.

Hieland Laddie, by Fred L. Morey.

The idea here embodied is of a peculiarly playful, quizzical character, yet not without tenderness and poetry; of genuine Scottish tone, reproduced with admirable fidelity in the music. It was at first suggested by a charmingly characteristic engraving.

A comely old lady, in the picturesque garb of the

Scotch peasant, sits just within the open doorway of a simple cottage; her neglected knitting and idle hands lie in her lap. Her head droops, and her eyes are closed. She is evidently napping. Prominent on the opposite wall, just facing her, hangs the portrait of a handsome youth, in the jaunty cap and gay plaid of the Highlander, his face and figure eloquent with health and strength and buoyant animation. From a certain resemblance in the woman's face, and the look of affectionate pride which it wears, it is evident that the picture is that of her own absent bonny boy, the subject of her last waking thoughts and present dreams. Entering the door from without, approaching swiftly but softly, so as not too soon to disturb her slumbers, comes the Highland Laddie himself, the living original of the picture, his eyes dancing with mischievous glee, as he steals forward, enjoying in advance her start and glad surprise when she wakes to find him whom she thought so distant close beside her.

The music is at once pleasing and graphic. The first strain should be played softly and gracefully, suggesting the dreams of the waiting mother; the second with more energy and decided contrasts, as if telling of her sudden awakening and startled surprise. Then the first strain repeats, stronger and more animated than before, and we may fancy her gaily recounting her dream to the returned wanderer. The third strain gives, in a mellow baritone melody, his answering voice; then one more subdued repetition of the first strain closes the composition, as with tranquil reflection on the remembered pleasure.

The peculiar Scotch inflection of the melody must

be brought out distinctly. Those familiar with *Robin Adair*, *Kelvin Green*, and similar Scotch songs, will at once recognize the slurred sixteenths on the first and fourth beats of many of the measures as characteristic of all Scotch music. These should be played precisely as the words "Highland Laddie" are pronounced, with a marked accent on the first syllable, gliding to the second, which is much lighter and detached from what follows. On this account the piece will be found an excellent study in rhythm.

Around the Maypole, Rustic Dance, by Fred L. Morey.

Among the most joyous and poetic of old English festivals was the annual celebration of May-day. The fairest maiden in the village was selected by her companions as Queen of the revels, crowned with May-flowers, and invested for the day with supreme authority. (See Tennyson's "May Queen.") Under her mild and mirthful sway, the young people abandoned themselves to every kind of innocent and jovial merry-making, till at evening, as culmination of the frolic, the flower-wreathed Maypole was erected in the centre of the village green, and around it all joined in the rustic dance, circling hand in hand, to the rollicking measures of pipe and fiddle. This composition is intended, as its name implies, to suggest such a scene, and express its merry mood. The melody and harmonies are purposely kept simple and unpretentious to fit the primitive, rural character of the festival; while the third, or Trio, strain, has a certain arch, capricious element, hinting of the playful coquetries of some village belle, or perhaps the May Queen herself.

The piece should be played at moderate tempo, with a bright, cheerful tone, crisp, distinct rhythm, and animated swing, as if to mark the time for the flying feet of the dancers around the Maypole.

Jumping Rope. Edw. Baxter Perry.

With a hop and a skip
Without stumble or trip
  My jump-rope I swing
  Keeping time while I sing.

The morning is bright
And my heart is so light
  For school doesn't keep
'Tis the first day of Spring.

This composition belongs to the class known as the graceful or playful lyric.

The mood expressed throughout is the exuberant light-hearted gaiety of the schoolgirl, out for a holiday in the breezy, exhilarating spring weather. It should be given with a rhythmic swing indicating the movement implied by the name, and with all the capricious abandon which the player can feel, remember, or imagine, in connection with the springtime and the days of youth, abounding health, and high spirits.

The Mermaid's Song, by Edward B. Perry.

The mermaid sits by the summer sea,
  At the evening hour and sings and calls,
The heart of the youth must break, Ah me!
  For it owns her power as the twilight falls.

The sea song blends with her tender sighs
　　As she lingers there while the west grows cold;
With the blue of the sea in her melting eyes
　　And a gleam in her hair like the sunset's gold.

The youth well knows he must say good night
　　To the world above and with her must go
With rapturous dread, and fearsome delight,
　　To a life of love in the depths below.

Let the melody in the right hand suggest the plaintive but sweetly seductive voice of the Mermaid, while the left-hand accompaniment rises and falls in gentle undulations, rippling and flowing like tranquil waves.

Undine, by Ferdinand Dewey.

This is named for that mythical water fairy of ancient legend who was the personification of all the delicate witchery of silver lake and stream, all the fleeting grace of those vague floating forms compounded of mist and moonlight, to which the primitive imagination of men attributed supernatural life, and all the wistful sadness of murmuring waves. She is said to have received or developed a human soul as the result of falling in love with a mortal, and when disappointed and cast off by her earthly lover, to have returned, without resentment or revenge, to endless sorrow and loneliness beneath the water. The gentle, touching sadness of the much-forgiving Undine breathes in the music of this simple little nocturne. The melody may be supposed to typify her plaintive yet winsome voice, while the flowing triplet accompaniment suggests the soft ripple of her native element. The composition will be found invaluable to teachers as an almost unequaled study in tone-production. It is hardly more than third grade in technical difficulty, so within the reach of the majority of pupils; yet musically it is sufficiently interesting to be used with far more advanced students who may need or enjoy something in the pure lyric vein. The melody is simplicity itself, yet warmly poetic and so clearly divided into short, easily grasped periods that it may be said to phrase itself. There are no tricky cadences to distract the attention of the player from the songful quality, and the left-hand accompaniment is unaffected and natural, affording no excuse for even momentary withdrawal of the mind from the quality and shading of the melodic phrases.

Danse Ecossaise, by Baker.

This is an attractive, melodious, though light and playful little work, of about third grade difficulty, popular with pupils, well put together, and a good rhythmic study, for it has the genuine characteristic Scotch lilt in its theme, namely, the short, unaccented note passing at once to a longer, sharply accented one, which is the distinguishing peculiarity, or the most noticeable one, in all Scotch melodies.

The harmonies are varied and pleasing, without being too complex for the average pupil, and it contains no dry sections and no tricky embellishments or cadenzas beyond the grade of the piece. As a whole, the mood is that of the joyous, frolicsome highland dance.

The Music Box, by Liebich.

The teacher will find in this musically rather trivial, but very realistic little composition, a valuable bit of most beneficial technical study, disguised under a sugar coating of surface prettiness and real graphic imitation, which will reach the interest and stimulate the work of certain pupils whom otherwise it may be hard to rouse.

It is a very excellent imitation of the sound of the old-fashioned music-box, and a piece of pronounced realism which they can fully understand, and the intended effects of which they can themselves clearly produce. This will often arouse the imagination and latent artistic perception of a young pupil who is wholly impervious to a deeper mood or thought.

It is the wedge that opens the way for better things; moreover, the child is getting a good étude for finger development without knowing it, which, as every teacher knows, is in some cases an important step in the right direction.

Titania, by Wely.

This little composition by the once great pianist is familiar to every teacher and well-nigh every pupil above the third-grade.

It has served as a sort of modest mile-stone on the path of pianistic progress for two generations, and still has its utilitarian value for students and its hosts of friends. It possesses some of the general qualities of the number by Liebich referred to; it is a good chromatic étude, well constructed and practically useful for technical purposes, but skilfully disguised and sugar-coated by means of a romantic name, and attractive melodic and descriptive characteristics. The ear of even the most superficial pupil is pleased, and his imagination awakened, while he is being adroitly stimulated to do willingly some otherwise distasteful work in the development of the much-needed finger facility so essential to the pianist.

We may fancy the scene suggested by the music as a secluded glade in the heart of the forest, half illuminated by the silvery moonlight, but encircled by the shadowy mystery of the woodland.

The introduction presents to us the capricious, mischievous, but daintily charming Titania, queen of the fairies. This should be played with extreme lightness and a playful coquettish freedom, to indicate her personality.

Then follows her graceful circling dance, as she weaves her spells and traces her mystic rings about the ancient oak in the centre of the glade, the silent witness of so many fairy revels in the past. This bright, airy dance movement should be given with the utmost speed compatible with accuracy, and with a clear, crisp, but always delicate touch.

The trio in B flat introduces a different mood and personage. His Fairy Majesty, king Oberon, emerges from the shadows in mock dignity, and half real, half-pretended displeasure, checks the dance by an imperious gesture, and proceeds to lecture his wayward wife for amusing herself so well in his absence. He scolds for a while, and then is mollified and won by her charms, and finally joins in the dance, which ends in a frolicsome burst of hilarity.

The marked contrast of this more grave and declamatory middle movement must be distinctly emphasized by means of a fuller tone, slower tempo, and more emphatic delivery.

The work is a simple but attractive picture in tone, devoid of any great depth or strength, but not without merit of its kind, and as a study possesses considerable technical value.

Heinrich Hofmann,
Aus Schöner Zeit.

This is another short and very beautiful lyric, of perhaps fourth-grade difficulty, in a sadly pensive mood. The name means literally, "Out of a beautiful time," but the idea for which it stands would be more aptly expressed in English by the words, "Sweet Memories." A German couplet stands as motto at the head of the music, suggesting its character and origin, which might be freely translated as follows: "By the door unheeded a zither swings, and the night wind sighs through its trembling strings."

The dream-picture called up both by the words and by the music may be something like this: A modest peasant's cottage in the forest of Tyrol; the home of childhood revisited in after years. Silence and loneliness reign in the familiar scene, where memories of departed loved ones wander like phantoms. By the open door hangs an old forgotten zither, its gay music

now stilled like the voices of the dear old home life of
the bygone years, but stirring dreamily in its sleep at
the caress of the night wind and recalling to the listener
who shall say what vague, far-away fancies and longings.
The strings murmur faintly, indistinctly, in sweet,
shifting harmonies, through which a plaintive strain of
melody is heard, like the echo of a beloved voice sounding through the halls of memory.

The whole effect should be subdued to the most
delicate of half-tones, and the accompaniment particularly must be a mere sigh of harmony.   There is
one rather unusual and tricky cadenza, but with carefully selected fingering it is by no means impracticable
even for moderately advanced players.

The Will O' the Wisp.

This name (which is synonymous with the French
feu follet and the German *Irrlichter*) is applied to those
wandering, elusive, phosphorescent lights which appear
by night in marshy meadows and damp forest glades,
and which have been, in all lands and ages, the source
of much wonder and curiosity and the origin of many
superstitious fears.   In Scotland they were formerly
called *death lights*, and their number, at any given time
or place, was supposed to indicate the number of
funeral candles that would be lighted in that community
during that year.

The Germans have a pretty legend that they are the
souls of candles prematurely extinguished, which fly
to these lonely places to live out the remainder of their
brief earthly existences, cut short by the cruelty or

carelessness of man; and that, in these fleeting hours of weird nocturnal revelry, they dance and sport together and amuse themselves by narrating to each other the scenes of human joy or sorrow which they illuminated during their short earthly lives.

This idea has been used by a number of composers as the subject of pianoforte compositions, the attempt being first to produce the realistic imitation in music of the dancing, flickering, mysteriously appearing and swiftly vanishing witch-lights against the dark background of the night; and second, in some cases, to suggest, in addition, the stories told by these spirit candles of the scenes they have witnessed, the ballroom gaiety or bridal happiness or burial rites upon which they have shone.

The subject is rich in varied possibilities which have, as yet, by no means been exhausted, though there are a number of compositions based upon it.

Probably the most difficult work of its length in existence is the Irrlichter by Liszt, one of his transcendental studies. A bright and pleasing, as well as useful, little piece for second-grade pupils, is the Will O' the Wisp by Jungman; a good, though simple embodiment of the idea, and a fine study in light, crisp, staccato playing.

The one by Jensen is somewhat more difficult, as well as more subtle musically. Both will be found of practical value to the student.

Inflection in Music.

NCIDENTALLY I wish here to call the attention of teachers with very young pupils to the set of easy and pleasing little pieces by Leibitz.

It will be found to be of value, not only in interesting the children, but in accustoming them to play simple melodies with some degree of intelligent expression and declamatory style. The melodies are literally fitted with words, which may be sung by the child if desired, and which serve not only to give a general idea of the character of the music and the way it should be played, but also to indicate where the heavy and light accents should properly fall. The child, when playing, thinks of the words and tries to make the notes say them; thus unconsciously getting the first elementary conception of inflection in melody playing; a most important, but often neglected element, popularly spoken of as ''the ability to make music talk,'' that is, to put some individual life and significance into it beyond what it is possible to indicate by the ordinary marks of expression.

No two consecutive notes of a melody should ever

be played exactly alike; for the measures, precisely like the lines in poetry, are subdivided into metrical feet, dactyls, trochees, &c., certain notes having more importance and demanding more stress or accent than others, like different words in a sentence or syllables in a word. This dynamic differentiation, properly observed, in a single simple phrase of music, makes all the distinction between mere machine playing and artistic delivery.

The little pieces referred to emphasize this point and render it clear to the child mind. They are a much-needed step in the right direction.

I would also mention as most useful in first grade work the set of pieces by J. M. Blose, Op. 15, which many teachers are finding invaluable.

Many more excellent things by American writers, for first and second grades, might be mentioned. I have no wish to discriminate, but lack of time and space, as well as of experience in this grade of work, prohibit my giving much attention to it in this volume.

Dance Forms

The Story of the Waltz.

VERY form of musical composition, and there are many such, which is primarily intended to accompany or suggest a certain definite physical action and movement, is logically developed from, and naturally grows out of, that movement itself.

The human body, with its infinitely varied possibilities of expression by means of attitudes, gestures, and movements, may be said to have been the first artistic instrument, and was used to convey ideas, emotions, and impressions through a universal and highly developed sign-language, long before speech was invented, and ages before modern fine arts were even dreamed of by the most visionary of prophets.

Men marched bravely and proudly to battle, expressing courage and defiance in every line and motion of their war-inspired figures; or slowly and dejectedly behind the bier of king or hero, expressing sorrow in every reluctant step and drooping pose, ages before the first band or even drum-corps headed the column.

Men danced the war dance, the love dance, the hunting and harvest and snake dances, and even the dance of religious frenzy, long before the first progressive

savage devised the rhythm-marking "tom-tom" to ani-
mate the dancers and heighten the effect.

The dance was first of all the arts, for it is an *art*,
when properly considered. It was the primitive but
accurate expression of life-experiences through motion.

Dance music consisted originally of merely a marked
rhythm, beaten out on some instrument of percussion,
some kind of drum, probably in the first instance a hol-
low log pounded with a club, this rhythm growing out
of, and demanded by the dance itself, and intended to
guide, control, and stimulate the dancers.

Little by little vocal cries were added, in time with
the dance and expressing its mood, the cry of pain, or
pleasure, or desire; the shout of triumph or defiance;
the wail of death-agony; the whoop of delirious frenzy.
These were gradually developed, refined, and combined
into increasingly expressive and beautiful melodic
phrases, till the song evolved from the dance.

The element of harmony was slowly added, and music
as an independent art was born with a body of beauty
and an immortal soul of emotional expression.

Every good dance form, however, even if not intended to accompany an actual dance, and no matter
how much it may be idealized, amplified, and elaborated,
must remain true in the main to its physical heredity
and antecedents; that is, it must be based upon the
rhythm and tempo, and express the general fundamental mood of the dance from which it springs;
though it may, and in modern times always does, add
many collateral and supplementary suggestions arising
out of, or conceivably incident to, the original dance.

The waltz is the *love-dance* of modern life, expressing

the romance, the poetry, the subtile glamour and fascination, of sex attraction, in its refined, idealistic, but irresistible potency.

In spite of much controversy there can be little doubt that it originated in Germany, as the name waltz, derived from the German word *walzen* (to turn or whirl), clearly indicates.

It was introduced into the social life of Vienna in 1780, and despite fierce opposition and abuse from certain quarters, soon gained a sure and permanent foothold in popular favor and spread its dominion throughout Europe, wellnigh supplanting most other dances, probably because of the universality and strength of the element which it embodies.

The most distinctive characteristic of the waltz, as a dance, is the complete isolation of the couples; and this is as it should be, symbolizing its significance.

In other dances, especially the older forms, the figures are executed by several couples, more or less collectively and interdependently. Partners are temporarily shifted; at times the evolutions are more complex and the social element more in evidence. In the waltz, each couple revolves in its own independent orbit, enveloped in its peculiar, exclusive atmosphere of swift, graceful motion, sensuous music, intimate mutual absorption, as much alone for the moment, in the midst of the whirling crowd, as if on a desert island. This is characteristic of the mood it is intended to express, and forms the most important element of fascination in this dance.

But in connection with this original, simple, concrete idea of the love-dance, many other subsidiary emotions and suggestions naturally arise, associated with it and incident to it, as, for example, the ardent wooing of the man, the gentle tenderness or the witching coquetry or playful mockery of the woman, the bitterness of misunderstanding, rebuff, and disappointment, the ecstasy of reunion after long parting, the fear and pain of impending separation, the anguish of a stolen farewell, the sudden, startling call "to arms," in the midst of the gaiety, the fateful, tragic message or ominous secret, imparted under cover of the jest and laughter of the ball-room. These and many more, of almost infinite variety, are possible accessory elements, which may interweave themselves with the simple pattern of the waltz as primarily conceived.

Waltz music, originally intended as an accompaniment and rhythmic guide to the dance, and concerned merely with the expression of the one simple idea, has gradually evolved and expanded so as to include and utilize all these secondary and incidental suggestions, till to-day the best waltzes are no longer strictly dance music, but complete, elaborate art works, tone pictures of ball-room scenes and moods, with the waltz movement and emotional motive as their principal theme, of course, but with all the intricate complexities of human life and passions vividly portrayed.

Among the light Viennese school of writers, catering to the rather trifling and frivolous taste of that second Paris, the crown as "waltz-king" was appropriated by the elder Strauss, and seemed likely to become hereditary in that family; and for actual dance purposes their waltzes remain to-day unequalled, strikingly rhythmic and enspiriting, embodying fully the sprightly grace, the languorous, half-artificial tenderness, the exaggerated, flirtatious spirit of the primitive waltz, at its first victorious entrance into the social centers of Europe.

The Strauss waltzes will always remain representative types of their class, but as genuine music they are of very "light weight" and have only very ephemeral value.

Even before their supremacy, Schubert and von Weber had raised the waltz into the realm of real music, developing and expanding its form, introducing into it the suggestive, descriptive, more profoundly emotional elements which gave to it a place among the distinct and recognized musical art forms.

Among their productions in this form Weber's "Invitation to the Dance" stands as the most remarkable, world-famous, and epoch-making example.

Then came Chopin, with his series of inimitable piano-forte waltzes, which will always remain standard classic types of this form, embodying, as they do, not only the fundamental idea of the waltz, in all its seductive grace and subtle tenderness and witchery, but also almost every possible shade and variety of mood, which might conceivably be experienced by the individual dancers under diverse conditions; from the heart-breaking sadness in the 'cello theme, forming the opening and principal subject in the little waltz in A minor, to the sparkling gaiety and frolicsome abandon of the joy-intoxicated *debutante* in the concert waltz

Most of the pieces described in this chapter will be found in Descriptive Analyses of Piano Works, by Edw. Baxter Perry.—ED.

in E flat major; from the manifold realistic as well as emotional suggestions in the waltz in A flat, founded upon Byron's "Battle of Waterloo," to the simple, naïve delight in rhythmic motion and innocent coquetry expressed in the little waltzes in G flat and D flat major, and the subtler, more exotic fascination of those in C sharp minor and B minor.

These waltzes will always be found invaluable studies for pupils of all grades above the second, for they include almost every variety of style and degree of difficulty, and are the best introduction to what has been aptly called "the true Chopinism of Chopin."

Schulhoff, Wieniawski, Rubinstein, Godard, and a host of others have contributed liberally and ably to this most popular form of idealized dance music, till it now offers to the pianist the richest, most varied selection of material for parlor or concert use of any of the dance forms, with the possible exception of the Polonaise. Its development may be said to have culminated with Moszkowski, whose four masterly waltzes for the piano, all concert numbers of some magnitude, fairly surpass all previous productions in ornate complexity of construction, in technical brilliancy, in wealth of musical and emotional content, and variety of fanciful suggestions. It is difficult to imagine their being excelled by any subsequent writer.

Just one word more concerning the subject matter of the waltz and its symbolic significance.

I repeat that it is openly and avowedly the *love dance* of modern civilization, based upon and expressing the mystery and magic of sex attraction.

Certain people are inclined to sneer at this emotion

and its use as an art subject.   Yet the fact remains that love, with its corollary emotions, is and must remain the oldest, most universal and most potent factor in human existence, the motive power in most important human actions, the determining element in most human experiences.   This fundamental truth has been recognized by all great authors from Shakespeare and Victor Hugo down.   Our musical critics may scoff if they choose, as indeed they sometimes do, at the idea that Chopin founded so colossal and dignified a work as his Sonata Op. 35, on what they are pleased to call "so trivial a subject as a love story."   But a theme of such vital and universal interest to the race, which has been deemed worthy to serve as the motive in nearly all the great dramas and works of fiction since literature began, may surely be legitimately utilized by the musician, and nowhere does it find more facile or diversified expression.

The Story of the March.

THE march is probably the oldest and certainly the most universally employed of all the forms of secular music. The name march is derived from the French word *marcher*, to step.

The distinctive rhythm of the march had its origin in the steady, authoritative beat of drums, cymbals, or tomtoms, accompanying and regulating the tread of moving bodies of foot soldiers, formerly spearmen and archers, later our modern infantry.

In process of time, to these instruments of percussion were added the trumpet, the fife, and in some instances the bagpipe, as in Scotland, supplementing the element of rhythm with that of melody of a stirring, inspiring character.

Then, little by little, as the desire for harmony developed, other instruments of deeper, more sonorous tone were introduced, like the horn and trombone, till the modern military band, composed of five varieties of brass instruments and four of wood-wind, came into being, in which, however, the drums still play an important part.

The practical use and importance of martial music,

especially the march, in all military manœuvres and on the field of battle, have been fully recognized by all army experts in all ages. Its purpose is two-fold:

First, to stimulate courage, ardor, and enthusiasm in the troops.

Second, to secure and facilitate concerted action, a regular, orderly, simultaneous movement of large bodies of men, by keeping them in step with a uniform, commanding rhythm, which spurs the laggard, checks the impatient, controls the rate of advance, and insures precision and mathematical certainty in the execution of army manœuvres. For this reason, a good band is as essential a part of a well-equipped regiment as its arms or ammunition-wagon.

There are three distinct types of the march in general use, among practically all nations, employed for different purposes and occasions, each having its own special characteristics and tempo.

First and most common, the ordinary parade march, leisurely, dignified, yet stirring, adapted to a rate of march of seventy-five steps a minute.

Second, the forced march or quickstep, more inspiring and exciting, with a tempo allowing for one hundred and eight steps to the minute.

Lastly, the storming march, the French *pas de charge*, with a hundred and twenty steps to the minute.

All these are distinctively military marches, actually or hypothetically used in connection with the various movements of troops.

In addition to them, there are the funeral march, slow, impressive, and mournful, and the wedding march, brilliant, joyous, and hopeful, with occasional touches of tender sentiment.

This wide diversity of mood and movement, possible within the legitimate limitations of the march, makes of it one of the broadest, most elastic forms of musical expression. The rhythmic tramp of marching feet must always serve as its basic idea, its physical germ, so to speak, out of which all other ideas suggested in it must be logically evolved, and to which they must all bear a definite relation.

But these secondary ideas and resultant moods may cover and include a vast range of thought and emotion.

For instance, men may march exultantly to victory, or sullenly to certain defeat; to the storming of a fortress, or in the feverish panic of a rout; to the coronation of an emperor, or the execution of a comrade; to a wedding or a funeral. All the emotions incident to these various occasions may be expressed in the music of the march.

As a definite, well-established musical form, recognized and adopted by all modern nations, the march reached its full development about the middle of the 18th century, since which time it has undergone few alterations, and fine specimens of every type of march are to be found in the writings of nearly all the leading composers from Handel to Wagner. It is always in two-four or four-four time, and is constructed on the following general plan:

First, an introduction of from four to sixteen measures, consisting mainly of a fanfare of trumpets, often, though not always, accompanied by drum effects.

This introduction, however, may be omitted, as is the case with most funeral marches. The first subject, or principal theme, is from sixteen to thirty-two measures in length, divided into distinct periods of four or eight measures, with no cadenzas or episodes of any kind to break the uniformity or interrupt the steady tramping of the rhythm. Then follows the second theme, most frequently in the dominant, and usually in a lighter, brighter vein, after which the first subject is repeated. Then comes a trio, more lyric in character, more quiet, and somewhat more slowly played, forming a marked and effective contrast with the opening movement, which is again repeated at the close of the work, with often a brief but brilliant coda or finale added. Technically speaking, this form is based upon that of the fully developed rondo, which, in its turn, had its origin in the Folk-song.

The Mendelssohn Wedding March.

No work of its kind is so familiar to the general public, throughout the civilized world, as the Wedding March by Mendelssohn. Since its creation, about eighty ago, it has been the one composition used at all weddings, where music had any part in the ceremony, and at how many thousands of weddings it has been heard, it would be impossible even to guess. No other march has ever been found so acceptable.

In stately city churches and simple village chapels, in hall and private parlor, in palace and cottage, from the eastern confines of Russia to far California, its jubilant, yet ideally lofty strains have voiced the

13

mood of the happy occasion for countless human hearts.

This march is a fragment, and the most familiar one, from Mendelssohn's music to "The Mid-Summer Night's Dream," an early but supremely able work, replete with delicate mysticism and dainty fairyland fancies, which accounts for the suggestions of that style apparent in it—notably in the trio. It was written to accompany the march of the noble wedding party in the play, a brilliant and joyous company, hence the atmosphere of pride and splendor as well as gaiety which envelops it. Those who would appreciate it fully should familiarize themselves with the scene in Shakespeare's drama. The work was written for orchestra, but there have been numerous piano arrangements.

The introduction gives us the gladsome bugle calls and trumpet signals which appear so often at the opening of march movements, as already stated; but in this case with no suggestion of the drums. The first movement, or subject, is proud, triumphant, exultant; telling of love the conqueror, of obstacles overcome, of happiness assured and imminent; while the trio, with its delicate trills and subtle wood-wind effects, hints of a background of shadowy woodland mystery, of fairy intrigue and influence, which color the whole texture of the story and are treated by Mendelssohn with a masterly finesse, which proves him to be peculiarly at home in that realm of fascinating unrealities.

The Bridal March from "Lohengrin," by Wagner.

In recent years this march has, to some small extent, encroached upon the universal supremacy in public favor formerly maintained by the Mendelssohn march. It is the only other famous wedding march, and is preferred by those who seek novelties and change in all the experiences of life, rather than the conservative, time-honored observances, and who specially affect the modern school in music. But there is a good and sufficient reason, inherent in the music, why this march will never supplant the one by Mendelssohn in general usage, a reason of which the public is not definitely conscious, but which is instinctively felt; namely, that it is not as broadly and fully adapted to any and every wedding occasion, is not as characteristically a wedding march in tone and mood.

The music is of a high grade of excellence, markedly rhythmic, simply melodious, and easily understood, also it is bright and joyous and so far well fitted for its purpose; but, like all of Wagner's music, it is exactly and exclusively adapted to the particular occasion and mood it was written to reflect. It is distinctively local in its coloring and, while perfectly in keeping with the scene for which it was intended, is not so generally in harmony with all occasions of the kind. It is designated as *Brautzug* (bridal train or march), and has special reference to the bride.

It accompanies Elsa and her bridesmaids in their progress from the palace to the chapel, where her wedding with Lohengrin is to take place, and portrays the personality of the innocent, white-souled, happy-hearted, but rather visionary, heroine; a type of delicately feminine but rather helpless maiden, of which Wagner was particularly fond in his early works—rather the modern German idea of maidenhood than the stronger and more heroic model, on which his later Brunhilde was moulded.

The music is light, tripping, daintily playful, but far from profound or serious. The mood it embodies is that of the fanciful girl, hardly more than a child, pleased and impressed by the pomp and glitter of the ceremony, the flowers and favors and bright costumes, and fascinated by the mystery of the future, but by no means realizing the intensely serious nature of the step she is taking. There is no touch of strong or deep emotion, or of vital reality, in these half-graceful, half-playful strains, and the usual tender trio is entirely lacking. While it is ideally beautiful and appropriate in its proper place, this march taken separately is obviously only a *fragment* and loses much of its charm and pertinence when parted from its proper setting and connection, like a section cut from some great picture.

The Dead March from "Saul," by Handel.

This short but characteristic funeral march, the first notable work of its kind, formerly universally known and much played, is rarely heard in our own day, though still familiar by name. It is an extract from

Handel's first great successful oratorio, which was first presented in London at King's Theatre, January 16, 1739.

The plot and text of the oratorio were based upon the well-known Bible narrative of Saul and David, and deal with the vicissitudes of Saul's reign, his wars, and intrigues; his relations with David, now friendly, now the reverse; and with the more than brotherly love of David and Jonathan. Its climax is reached with the death of Saul and Jonathan in the battle with the Philistines, and David's lament for their loss, especially for the latter.

"The Dead March," as it is called, symbolizes the fall of the king and prince, as well as the crushing defeat of the Jews, the grief of the nation, and David's deep personal sorrow for his lost friend.

The emotional motives of the march are to be traced to two familiar quotations from David's lamentation.

"How are the mighty fallen in the midst of the battle!"

"I am distressed for thee, my brother Jonathan. Very pleasant hast thou been unto me; thy love to me was wonderful, passing the love of women. How are the mighty fallen!"

Their expression in the music, when regarded from our modern standpoint, and compared with similar efforts by a Chopin or a Wagner, is decidedly primitive and inadequate—not to say commonplace.

The very tonality selected is wholly inappropriate according to every law of æsthetics, the work being in C major, the only funeral march in existence, so far as known to the writer, entirely in a major key.

But it must be remembered that the piano score gives a very imperfect idea of the orchestral effect; also that it was at a time when music, as a medium of emotional expression, was still in its infancy; its material, like that of the English language in the time of Chaucer, still in process of formation, its resources scarcely even guessed at by the best musicians.

This march is one of the earliest steps in the development of tonal art, and as such deserves our respect. Moreover, though antiquated in style, and meager in the means employed, it possesses a certain simple dignity and directness, not without impressiveness. It furnishes a good example of the effective massing of the solid, if common, harmonies, imposing in their grave simplicity, characteristic of all Handel's larger works.

FUNERAL MARCH, BY CHOPIN.

I.

Bells that toll o'er a nation's tomb,
Solemn, slow, as the knell of doom,
Dirge, that voices a dawnless gloom,
    Poland's woes lamenting.
Strong as rage for a loved one slain,
Strong as hearts that exult in pain,
Daring death though the cause be **vain,**
    Poland's wrongs resenting.

II.

Sad as tears for a nation shed,
Sad as dreams of a hope that's **fled,**
Sad as thoughts of our long-lost **dead,**
    Still for Poland sighing.
Brave as blades that in stern delight,
Flash and fall in the van of fight,
Keen for vengeance and for the right
    Poland's foes defying.

* The famous Funeral March by Beethoven is a part of **his** Sonata Op. 26, fully described in "Descriptive Analyses"

III.

Then a strain, like a tender prayer
Welling up from a soul's despair,
Suppliant sigh for a land once fair,
    Heavenward now ascending.
Sobbing strain with passionate swell,
Striving still of the past to tell,
Ere their bravest and noblest fell,
    Poland's life defending.

IV.

Then once more with relentless weight,
Crushing chords like the voice of fate,
Speak in dissonance desolate,
    Wrath and anguish blended.
Sad and slow let the cadence fall,
Sombre, soft, like a velvet pall,
Silent darkness is over all,
    Poland's pain is ended.
        —E. B. P., March, 1897.

Chopin's Funeral March.

This composition, unquestionably the best funeral march yet written for the piano, originally appeared as the third movement in Chopin's great, dramatic, allegorical tone-poem, the Sonata in B flat minor, Op. 35.

It is, however, a very complete and powerful work in itself, and is published and most often played separately, the whole sonata being too difficult for any but the most advanced pianists.

A full analysis of the sonata, with the interesting Polish narrative on which it is founded, as well as the allegorical significance of both, may be found in my volume of "Descriptive Analyses of Piano Works."

Taken independently, this march is the strongest and noblest expression of profound and passionate sorrow, as well as the most perfect type of its kind to be found in piano literature.

It is supposed to accompany the march of the funeral procession bearing the bride and heroine of the story to her last long rest. It begins with the distant muffled tolling of funeral bells, then the solemn, heart-breaking music grows gradually stronger as the procession draws nearer, taking on more and more the inflexible tramping cadence of the funeral march, with an occasional suggestion of muffled drums, rising at last to a stupendous climax of pain and despair, then pausing by the open tomb.

Next follows an exquisitely tender and touching little Trio, in D flat major, sweet and simple as the song of a child, symbolizing prayer at the grave, thrilling with tearful memories of happier days. Then in heavy, crashing chords, inexorable as the voice of fate, the march movement is resumed, slowly diminishing, dying into silence, as the black-robed procession of mourners return to the village, their last sad offices completed.

The bride in this story is an allegorical personification of Poland, so fondly loved and bitterly lamented, and the grief and despair are for the death of a nation, expressed with a passionate intensity, and yet with a strength and nobility of utterance rarely equalled and never surpassed, even by Chopin.

Regarded from a technical standpoint, the march is not difficult, but it demands an emotional capacity and insight, as well as a command of tone quality, possessed by few players, and it is often atrociously murdered, even by our leading concert pianists.

Marche Militaire, by Schubert.

This is another world-famous march used in many lands and in many forms and arrangements. It is scored for brass band and orchestra, also as a piano solo and four-hand arrangement, as well as a brilliant concert number in Tausig's superb paraphrase. It is always enjoyed and admired (in spite of being almost hackneyed) for its freshness and sparkling vitality, its irresistible, rhythmic swing, its simple, beautiful, spontaneous melodies, as clear as crystal, as bright as sunlight on steel.

It is a perfect example in form, content, and mood, of the parade march, not rapid, but pompous, splendid, full of martial spirit.

This march was written in honor of the Austrian Imperial body-guard, a crack regiment of grenadiers or heavy infantry, officered by some of the highest nobles of the realm—a proud, dashing set of blades.

The ranks were composed of picked men, selected for their lofty stature and stalwart proportions. They were superbly uniformed, wearing glittering helmets, breast plates, and back pieces of polished steel, and were drilled to the last degree of military precision. The regiment was maintained as much for display on state occasions, to add pomp and splendor to court functions, as for service in the field in time of need. They were supposed to be invincible in war, and known to be so with the ladies at home.

The music, written as a compliment to them, expresses the spirit of this martial body, and conveys the impression which their appearance in line of march was calculated to produce.

It opens with an ingenious introduction of six measures, giving, even in the piano score, a distinct suggestion of the beat of drums in reiterated chords in the right hand, exactly reproducing the most common and simple rhythm employed by the drummers at the beginning of so many marches—a rhythm familiar to every schoolboy in every land, and imitated by every boy that ever marched with a wooden gun. Interwoven with this is a stirring trumpet call, a ringing summons to war and victory.

Then comes the march proper, stirring, brilliant, with its catchy melody and swinging rhythm, growing stronger and louder as the parade draws nearer.

The light, dainty, almost playful Trio in the subdominant suggests the grace, beauty, and gaiety of the fair spectators crowding windows and balconies to witness the passing pageant, with flutter of fans and kerchiefs, scattering smiles and glances and bouquets upon the favorite officers as they pass.

Then a sonorous repetition of the first movement closes this march, which will live as long as "Schubert, the melodious" holds any place in the memory of the musical world.

Rakoczy March (Pronounced Rah-kow'-tsee), by Franz Liszt.

This is one of the most stirring and spirited concert marches in the repertoire of the modern pianist. It is generally attributed to Liszt, because chiefly known in his version of it for the piano, but it is, in reality, much older than Liszt's time, and is one of the many fragments of wild, original, gipsy music rescued by him from oblivion, and revivified for the musical world of our day in his masterly adaptation for the piano. Its authorship is anonymous, but it was composed (one can not say written, as they never wrote anything) by one of those gifted but unknown gipsy musicians, who were for a time so closely identified with the social life of Hungary in the palmy days of her independence and prosperity. They were, in a sense, adopted as the national musicians, were the special *protégés* of the court and the great nobles, and from them comes all the so-called Hungarian music, though they were of a totally different race.

Rakoczy was a famous Hungarian general and patriot in the days of her long, desperate struggle for continued independence, of whose daring ability and phenomenal achievements fabulous tales are told. This march was composed in his honor, named for him and dedicated to him, and is a splendid tribute to his memory.

It is a "storming march," fierce, yet sombre, full of barbaric, half-fanatical patriotism and the lust of battle.

It celebrates the swift marches through the gloom of mighty forests, the midnight attacks, the resistless charges and the sudden tempests of death and flame descending upon the sleeping foe, which made Rakoczy, at the head of his wild riders, the terror of the invader and the idolized hero of his people. The mood is impetuous, uncompromising, darkly exultant, the very spirit of the night attack, the delirious Berserk frenzy of the charge expressed in startlingly weird harmonies, full of the rattle of the war-drums and the ring of brazen trumpets and dissonant clank of contending hosts.

This march is to be found in various arrangements for the piano, the most complete and stupendous being the Fifteenth Hungarian Rhapsody; but there are also several more or less simplified editions, and it has been effectively scored for both band and orchestra.

Other famous marches of more modern times are "The Turkish Grand March," by Beethoven, from "The Ruins of Athens," and "The Tannhaeuser March," by Wagner; both described in detail in my volume of Descriptive Analyses already referred to.

The Story of the Polonaise.

HIS distinctively Polish musical form, which has been so closely identified with Poland's history through all her manifold vicissitudes during more than three centuries, originated in 1573 in Cracow, then the Polish capital, on the occasion of the coronation of the young French prince, Henri d'Anjou, as king of Poland.

The great nobles, always, unfortunately, at feud among themselves, which was ultimately the cause of Poland's downfall, were wholly unable to agree upon one of their own number to fill the throne left vacant by the death of the last of the Jagiellos, and finally united in electing the young prince to the office, which was intended to be little more than that of a figurehead to the ship of state.

The coronation ceremony, which took place in October of that year, was one of the most magnificent affairs ever witnessed, for Poland was then at the height of her power, wealth, and splendor, and barbarically oriental in her love of lavish display and extravagant personal adornment.

It was no uncommon thing for a knight to wear the

entire value of his estates and possessions in jewels at a court function.

One of the important features of this grand festival was a presentation ceremony to introduce the members of the court and aristocracy to the new king, a reception of regal proportions.

All the great lords and ladies of the realm, arrayed in their most sumptuous apparel, with all the available jewels in evidence, assembled in one of the lower halls in the royal castle, formed in a glittering procession, marched in stately pomp up the grand staircase, through various halls, galleries, and ante-chambers, finally up the length of the vast magnificent throne-hall to the daïs, where the king awaited them, there to be presented to his majesty by the grand master of ceremonies.   This march was accompanied by suitable music written for the occasion by a local composer; music intended not only to mark the rhythm of the march, but to add to the pomp and pride and beauty of the occasion, and to embody the peculiar racial characteristics and national traits of the Poles, thus in a way supplementing the introductory feature.

It was a musical presentation of the Polish people to their new monarch.   Then and there was born the Polonaise, which, from that germ, crude and primitive though it may have been, has gradually developed into a definite, complete, and quite elaborate musical form, recognized and used the world over, the common property of all composers.

But the true Polonaise, no matter when, where or by whom it may be written, manifests distinct traces of its original heredity, natal environment, and early associations; always "harks back," so to speak, to those olden days of Polish pomp and splendor, is always Slavonic in its general tone, and aristocratic in its manner and mood.

Its distinguishing rhythm is a measure of six eighths, though sometimes written in three-four time, of which the second eighth is divided into two sixteenths.   It is always a promenade march, not a dance.   In later times it was used as the opening number at state balls at court and at the palaces of the nobles, not only in Poland, but, to some extent, in other lands, but has always retained its original characteristics even to the present day, though it is now used rather as a musical art form than as a familiar feature of the modern ball. Precisely as in the case of the waltz, however, as time went on, the music of the Polonaise was broadened and elaborated so as to include in its scope the expression not only of the original mood and scene, but additional ideas, feelings and fancies, even incidents connected with or arising out of it.

For example, one may recall the days of Poland's glory with very widely different emotions; with pride and exultation over her past; with heart-breaking sorrow at her present degradation; with tearful sympathy for her wrongs and sufferings; with bitter indignation against her oppressors.   Any of these moods, as well as many others, may be legitimately expressed in the Polonaise.

Chopin, in whose hands the Polonaise reached its highest development and perfection, has given us a great variety of moods and suggestions, all based on the original Polonaise idea and embodied in that form.

They are all ideal Polonaises, but no two of them are alike in emotional content.

The Military Polonaise, Op. 40, No. 1, Chopin.

In his Military Polonaise, Opus 40, No. 1, which is perhaps the best known, he tells us of the martial spirit and prowess, the courage and chivalry of the Polish knights in their magnificent, gem-studded armor, sweeping the field of battle on their matchless steeds, with the clash of steel, the blast of trumpets, bearing the Polish standard to victory.

Polonaise in C Minor, Op. 40, No. 2, Chopin.

The Polonaise in C minor, Op. 40, No. 2, is a broad, noble, but profoundly gloomy work of the darkly majestic type.

The theme, in octaves, voices the stern, well-nigh despairing indignation of a strong, dauntless race, crushed to earth by the overwhelming weight of numbers, but sullenly biding its time, and gathering the remnant of its strength for one last desperate struggle, heroic, though hopeless, to avenge its many bitter wrongs; with pride and courage still unbroken, but with a full realization of its impotence.

It is the same spirit that led the Polish students in the streets of Warsaw to throw themselves unarmed upon the Russian bayonets by the hundreds, preferring a futile death to a life of shame among a vanquished people.

The lighter, more capricious trio, with its occasional brief touches of plaintive tenderness, suggests a fleeting thought, half pathetic, half satirical, of the days that "might have been."

Polonaise in C sharp Minor, Chopin.

No Polonaise is a greater favorite, especially among those who incline towards the lyric style in music, than that in C sharp minor, on account of its great variety and markedly poetic mood. It opens with a bold, heroic introduction, expressing the martial, defiant spirit of the Polish cavaliers, then changes abruptly to a tender lyric strain, suggesting the grace and charm and delicate beauty of the "eternal feminine," never and nowhere more potent than in the chivalric days of Poland's power and splendor.

Then follows a brief but strong and masterly climax in a somberly dramatic mood, beginning with a whispered hint of gloom and mystery and impending danger, then rising suddenly through a series of sequences to a crash of minor and diminished harmonies, thrillingly significant of the sudden shock of conflict. Then a radical transition to an exquisitely sweet and tender strain, breathing of love and romance, like a sudden gleam of sunlight through the storm clouds.

The trio is an intensely impassioned duet between the knight and his lady, full of Slavonic fervor, yet vibrant with an almost desperate sorrow, the reflex of the omnipresent dangers and strife through which the path of true love must lead, too often, to bitter partings and into the shadow of sudden death.

14

The composition is less of a Polonaise in the strict
sense than a picture of Polish life which the Polonaise
calls before the mind.

Polonaise, Op. 26, No. 2, Chopin.

A notably original and weirdly fascinating work by
Chopin in Polonaise form is the one in E flat minor.
It opens with a curious fantastic movement, darkly
tragic in mood, indeed voicing a shuddering despair
too black and terrible to be attractive to the majority
of young players, which is probably the reason why the
work, though extremely interesting and of only moderate difficulty, is very little used.

One of Chopin's compatriots states that this first
strain is intended to imitate the doleful clank of the
chains upon the vanquished Polish patriots in their long
march to Siberia.

It is followed by a long, reiterated and insistent movement in choral form and unequivocally religious vein,
a suggestion of the pathetic attempt of hearts crushed
by defeat, smarting with injustice and humiliation, tor-
tured by keenest personal grief, striving to find comfort
and consolation in the promises of faith.

Andante Spianato and Polonaise, Op. 22, Chopin.

One of the very best and also one of the most difficult and brilliant of the Chopin Polonaises is the one
in E flat, usually designated by the above title.

The Andante Spianato is simply a quiet introduction

prefixed to the Polonaise proper, *spianato* being an Italian word not often used in musical terminology, which means *tranquil*, and qualifies *andante*. It has no reference to *spinning*, as has been inferred by some on account of the name and the character of the accompaniment.

This movement is a tender lyric in Chopin's sweetest, most exquisite vein, ornamented by a series of delicate embellishments.

It appears to be a sort of waking dream, indulged in by the young composer at the moment of the creation of this great Polonaise, when his thought and fancy were engrossed with the life-history and characteristics of his beloved country. A dream of those happier days, long past, touched by a transient gleam of hope that they might return. The whole work belongs to his early, more optimistic period before he was twenty, before his long exile had begun, before Constantia had broken his heart and shattered his ideals, before his home had been sacked and burned by the Russians, the period of youth and hope and aspiration, when life still glowed with the rosy tints of dawn. Then a sudden blast of trumpets and crash of cymbals recall us to the gorgeous court pageant of 1573, heretofore described, announcing that royalty has taken its seat in the great hall, the ceremony has begun, and the splendid procession may start on its imposing march. Then comes the Polonaise, brilliant, stirring, triumphant, replete with a wealth of constantly varying melody, rich in harmonic coloring, well-nigh overladen with embellishment, like the costumes of the lords and ladies who defile in a glittering line before the eyes of our fancy; superb knights in jewel-studded armor, beautiful ladies in silk and velvet of every hue, flashing with gems.

From moment to moment the music changes in character to suggest the shifting kaleidoscopic impressions produced by this moving pageant, now bold and proud and martial, now tender and graceful, again playful, coquettish or impassioned, while the procession winds on up the grand staircase and across the magnificent throne hall.

Now and then a sharp dissonant clash of steel on steel indicates the salute of the knights to their new monarch with the war-like din of sword on shield.*

Polonaise in E Major, by Franz Liszt.

Among the well-nigh innumerable Polonaises of every degree of merit and difficulty, written by different composers of various lands and periods, this in E major, by Liszt, is probably the best, aside from those by Chopin, and it is certainly the most widely known. It is a standard concert number the world over; a work of the first magnitude in breadth, musical significance, and technical difficulty, and it is the only one within the writer's acquaintance in which identically the same theme is made to serve both as first subject and as trio melody. This is a unique conceit, and carried out with Liszt's own clever ingenuity.

The idea is to suggest the distinctive traits and characteristic attributes of the Polish race, manifested under the modifying influence and conditions of sex. In other

* The greatest of the Chopin Polonaises, the Op. 53, is a standard concert number with all pianists, and is fully analyzed in "Descriptive Analysis" by same author.

words, the racial temperament in its masculine and feminine embodiment. The characteristic theme symbolizes the national spirit, remaining essentially and fundamentally the same in both cases, while the widely varying treatment and setting clearly differentiate between the sexes in which it finds embodiment.

In the first subject this theme appears in bold, forceful chords, instinct with a resolute, martial spirit, with the pride, heroic courage and fierce joy in conflict, typical of the dashing steel-clad cavalier.

In the trio it reappears note for note, but in a higher register, treated in light, delicate, playful mood, with a highly elaborate and ornate setting, sparkling with dainty embellishments, to represent the feminine incarnation of the Polish racial type, the charming, capriciously brilliant, witchingly winsome Polish lady.

Even the musically untrained ear may easily learn to follow this dominant theme through all its modifications and transmigrations, and enjoy its varied poetic suggestions, as well as its tonal fascination; while to the student of the art it is a most interesting example of musical symbolism.

The second subject, in heavy, rugged chords and octaves, is in the style of Liszt, rather than Polish— the Hungarian point of view—vigorous, but a little pompous and supercilious.

It may be supposed to represent the rough, wild, primitive conditions of those early days on the eastern frontier of civilization, when the strong arm was the only law and logic, and the good sword the only arbitration.

Polonaise, by E. A. MacDowell.

There has been one, and only one, Polonaise written on this side the Atlantic which fully deserves to rank with the masterpieces in this form by the Old-World composers, namely, that by MacDowell.

Though not of extreme difficulty, in fact, within the possible playing repertoire of most fairly advanced amateurs, it is a broad, effective concert number, worthy of a place on any artist's program, and far less used than it should be.

Its opening theme is markedly original, yet thoroughly characteristic of the Polonaise, conceived in its gloomily retrospective mood. Its sombre majesty and forceful intensity bring irresistibly to the mind the dark, tragic history, the desperate heroism, the gallant but futile struggle, and the ultimate hapless doom of a proud and noble race.

It is a stern, indignant protest against tyranny, injustice, and cruelty, as strongly and feelingly expressed as if MacDowell had himself been a native son of Poland, with an undertone of fatalism eminently in keeping with the Slavonic temperament. In fact it always recalls to me those wonderful lines of Swinburne:

> More dark than a dead world's tomb,
> More deep than the great sea's womb,
> Fate.

The *trio*, as is customary in the polonaise, introduces a suggestion of a lighter, more playful vein. It is bright, vivacious, almost humorous, indicating a brief abandonment to an almost reckless gaiety on the very verge of the disaster which is recognized as inevitable, yet is ignored, even scouted for the moment, with that incredible courage and half frivolous, half cynical humor, characteristic alike of the French and Polish nobility, even on the way to the guillotine, or that far more terrible living death, Siberian exile.

This trio closely imitates, in mood and style, the music of the Hungarian Gipsies; indeed, one might easily fancy it to be of Hungarian origin.

This peculiar touch is a rather unusual and daring innovation in the Polonaise, but is entirely legitimate and appropriate, as will be understood when it is remembered that those musical nomads from across the Hungarian border were often engaged at the castles of the Polish grandees to furnish the music for their balls and festivals, and were, of course, often called upon, as we may assume to be the case in this instance, to accompany the brilliant, stately march of the Polonaise. The long, wild, sweeping cadenza, which leads back to the first theme, is unmistakably symbolic of the rush and roar of the bitter winter wind from the northern steppes, raging about the castle walls, moaning dismally among the towers and battlements—the ominous voice of Nature allegorically significant, perhaps, of the rushing wings of death and destruction so imminently impending.

The Story of the Gavotte.

HE Gavotte is an antique French dance named for the Gavots, or people of the *pays de Gap*, a province in southeastern France, now forming a part of Dauphiné.

This slow, grave, but pompous dance was for generations the special possession and pride of the peasants of that section, forming a part of all their rustic merry makings, wedding festivals, and the like.

It is in common time, beginning always on the third beat of the measure, with a strong accent on the first of those following.

Its strongly marked rhythm and its mood of heavy gaiety, and rather bombastic dignity, indicate the strength and energy, the latent martial spirit, and the somewhat exaggerated pride and self-complacency of the peasantry of southern France, whose character is far more akin to the fiery yet taciturn Spanish mountaineers than to that of the flippant Parisian populace. In fact, there is a tradition not fully authenticated, but plausible, and seemingly borne out by the style of the music, that the Gavotte was imported across the Pyrenees from Spain, where, in earlier times, it figured as a sword dance, in which only the men-at-arms participated, the rhythm being marked by the clash of sword on shield.

As a musical form it reached its full development and general recognition in the days of Bach, who used it frequently in his various suites.

Perhaps the best known and most usable of the Bach gavottes are the one in G minor from his English Suite and the transcription by Saint-Saëns of his gavotte in B minor, originally written for violin.

In modern times, no Gavotte has been so universally popular as that in E minor, by Silas. It is a strikingly spirited and characteristic composition, evidently based on the idea of the original use of the Gavotte as a Spanish sword dance, just referred to.

The first and second subjects give the martial spirit and splendor of the Spanish tourney, the clash of steel, the flash and glitter of swift sword play; while the trio in E major introduces what appears to be a dialogue in duet form, between one of the swordsmen and a lady among the spectators.

This is a charming bit of melodic writing and a fine example of simple, but thoroughly musical counterpoint.

For teaching material in this line I would refer the reader to the "Gavotte Imperial" by Morey, elsewhere mentioned in these pages, also the excellent and comparatively easy Gavotte in F sharp minor, by Orth. The "Gavotte Moderne" by Liebling, a most original and effective work, and the brilliant Gavotte by D'Albert from his Suite for piano, are available for pupils above the fourth grade.

Story of the Tarantelle.

THIS fierce, fiery, and exceedingly rapid dance, indigenous to southern Spain and Italy, but now cultivated and popular in all lands, as a definite and recognized musical form, originated in an ancient and widely prevalent belief, or legend, among the credulous peasants, concerning the bite of the tarantula. It was supposed that the venom of this spider, which is in most cases fatal to the victim, produced in him a delirious mania for dancing, which must be indulged and encouraged to the utmost as the only possible means of saving his life. The excitement and violent exercise of the dances produced profuse perspiration, thus lessening the fever and aiding nature in the effort to throw off the poison.

When any one of their number was bitten, it was customary for the peasants of the village or country-side to assemble in haste, form a ring and take turns in dancing with the poor wretch, till each became weary and gave place to the next.

The dancers were stimulated to their utmost speed and to a perfect frenzy of excitement, by the wildest, fastest music which could be produced, and by the frantic shouts and applause of the spectators, till at last the victim dropped in complete exhaustion. This dance was called "The Tarantella," and its half-delirious excitation appealed so strongly to the fiery temperament of the south that it was gradually adopted as a local feature of village festivals and country fetes, without the physical necessity which first produced it; and the accompanying music crystallized into a definite form, with a distinctive character and rhythm, which is now known and used the world over.

It is always a prestissimo movement, having no trio or lyric theme of any kind, and usually, though not invariably, in a minor key. It is, of course, always stirring and impetuous to the last degree, with strongly marked rhythmic effects suggesting its original spirit and purpose.

The best specimens of this form, within the writer's acquaintance, for use with pupils of third and fourth grades, are the well-known Tarantelle in A flat, by Heller, and the less familiar but equally effective Tarantelle in A minor by Thorne.

Pupils should be told the story of the origin and purpose of the dance, and encouraged to feel and express its wild mood and feverish excitement.

For more advanced students I would suggest, as fine studies and telling numbers for public use, the Tarantelle by Fred L. Morey, and the Tarantelle by S. B. Whitney, also that by Gustave Schumann (not Robert). Perhaps the best recent contribution to piano literature, in this form, is the Tarantelle by A. G. Salmon. Among other noted Tarantelles are those of Franz Liszt, Joachim Raff, and L. B. Mills. A little Tarantelle in A Minor by Pieczonka has met with immense favor in America. Closely allied to the Tarantelle is the Saltarelle and the Farandole; a popular example of the latter is the well-known composition of Raoul Pugno.

As all musicians know, the greatest Tarantelles are those by Chopin and Liszt, but they are concert numbers and technically too difficult for any but the most advanced students.

The Story of the Minuet.

THIS ancient, dignified, and stately dance is supposed by many to have originated in England, in fact is often spoken of as an "old English dance," because it was much in vogue and a universal favorite in England in former days, especially during the eighteenth century, and because it seems peculiarly suited to the elegant and polished but rather punctiliously formal customs and atmosphere of English social life at that period. It is closely identified in our minds with the sumptuous drawing rooms, the elaborate costumes, the exaggerated, often stilted courtesy of intercourse in those olden days in England, and even in our own country in Colonial times; with powder, patches and point-lace ruffles, with curled wigs and velvet "small-clothes" and gold-hilted rapiers; with the days when a gentleman turned an epigram or the point of his antagonist's sword with the same smiling nonchalance.

The true minuet is fairly redolent of lavender-scented snuff and mint julep, so much is it a part of the old régime, but in reality it is English only by adoption and inherent fitness. It originated in the French **province of Poitou the middle of the 17th century.**

Its name is derived from *menu*, meaning small, as the steps of the dance were short and mincing. Its distinguishing characteristic was a slow, stately grace.

As a dance, for practical ball-room use, it went out of vogue in our grandmothers' time and is now rarely seen except on the stage; but as a musical form, unlike most of the obsolete dances, it still holds a certain place in popular favor, even in our day

It was much used by Bach, Handel, Haydn and Mozart and reached its highest development in the hands of Beethoven.

But an occasional belated, sporadic, but perfect and beautiful blossom of this form appears among the modern works of living writers, side by side with the waltz and the descriptive fantasy, like the old-fashioned primrose and hollyhock in the midst of the latest products of horticulture.

The Minuet is generally written in $\frac{3}{4}$, though sometimes in $\frac{3}{8}$ time.

The first subject consists of two periods, usually of eight bars, followed by a second subject, practically a second minuet, of a more quiet, lyric character, forming a contrast with the first, after which the first subject is repeated.

This second contrasting strain, of which there are sometimes more than one, alternating with repetitions of the first section, is called a Trio, not only in the minuet, but in marches and all other dance music, and an explanation of this term may be in place here; for though in general use, it seems to be little understood by the average student.

A Trio meant originally a composition for three instruments, and these more quiet, contrasting, middle movements in the various dance forms, such as the Minuet, the Gavotte, etc., were at first written for only three voices, or in three-part harmony.

Later this restriction was abandoned, but the name and general character of the movement were retained. Hence we speak of the Trio of a dance or even of an Impromptu, though the entire work is played upon a solo instrument like the piano.

Considered as a musical art form, the Minuet, like every other dance, must conform to the rhythm and general character, and express the usually prevalent mood, of the special type of actual dance, out of which it grew, but as explained in connection with the waltz and other dances, it may also incidentally express, in addition to this fundamental idea, any emotion, fancy, thought, or even action, which might naturally be attributed to any one or more of the dancers during their participation in it, or be suggested by the time and scene; hence its scope, in spite of seeming limitations, is quite varied and extensive.

We find, indeed, that the Minuet changes materially in tone, with the passing of the years, reflecting the temper of the times in which it was produced, and the personality of the different composers. In the hands of Bach and Handel it was stately and pompous, but cold and rigidly formal; in those of Haydn it became more cheerful, even brightly playful. Mozart gave it a more graceful, tender and dreamy character; while Beethoven, in many of his minuets, made open sport of the prim, straight-laced formalism of the old days, giving to them a decided flavor of rough and rugged humor. In fact, with him the Minuet evolved into the modern Scherzo.

The following are some of the best known and most interesting Minuets now in general use for teaching purposes:

Minuet by Boccherini.

This is an old, but still popular and attractive number, of moderate difficulty, with an exquisite sensuous melody, and a captivating rhythmic swing, expressing chiefly the languorous grace and tender witcheries of the fair daughters of the sunny south, for whom the stately figures of the Minuet served as a fitting field of conquest, an appropriate setting for their charms. Of all Minuets now in use, this is the most in harmony with the spirit of the dance as used in Italy. The red blood and the rich red wine of the south are in it. We cannot but associate it with the sumptuous, pleasure-loving lives of the old Venetian and Florentine nobility.

Minuet in B Minor by Schubert.

This is a work of greater strength and more marked contrasts than the foregoing, vigorously Teutonic in character, containing two markedly different elements. The first subject, in octaves and chords, is bold, vigorous, almost stern in character, yet with a certain rugged gravity. It reminds one of some old feudal war baron of medieval days, more wonted to camps and fields of strife than to the ladies' hall, yet striving with a sort of half grim, half humorous solemnity, to tone down his rough manners and moderate his martial stride, in keeping with the decorous demands of the occasion and the movements of the dance.

The graceful melodious trio portrays his partner, a sprightly, winsome maiden in all her festive finery of silk and lace and jewels, with a touch of playful coquetry in her smile. The personality is piquante, yet tender and charming. The two form a most effective contrast.

The Minuet by Paderewski.

The most popular minuet of the present time for the piano the world over is the one in G major by Paderewski, partly because of the fame of its composer, and partly because of its own intrinsic merit. It is light, graceful, and pleasing, rather than markedly strong or original, and is doubtless the more of a universal favorite for that reason. The melodies are extremely simple and easily grasped, though attractive, and the harmonies are based mainly upon the tonic and dominant seventh chords. The cadenzas are sparkling and effective, but not especially difficult; hence it is a useful and available study for pupils of even the fourth grade.

It is distinctly a Minuet *à la Française*, best characterized, perhaps, by the word *charming*. The Slavonic temperament, in its lighter moods, is more closely akin to the French than to that of any other race, and it is a significant fact that the French language, French thought, and French social customs and fashions have been predominant in the higher circles in Poland and Russia for more than a century.

15

It is not surprising, therefore, that Paderewski, who is Polish by birth and nature, but largely French by education, long residence, and at least superficial predilections, should have given us a Minuet which, in spite of its modern hybrid origin, "reverted to type," as the scientists say, that is, returned to the original French ideal and spirit.   In listening to the spirited yet polished phrases of this music, in which playful vivacity and refined elegance are so equally blended, one may easily fancy himself back in the days of Louis XV, amid the glitter and gaiety of the court ball-room, where the sparkle of lights and jewels is matched by the scintillations of wit and repartee; where clever epigrams and florid compliment are bandied back and forth with swift, accustomed skill, like balls in a tennis court, while gallant cavaliers lead their fair partners through the mazes of the dance, to the throbbing music of flutes and violins, which covers the whispered interchange of the fleeting sentiment, born of the hour and scene, half jest, half serious.

The composition should be played at a very moderate tempo, with a certain capricious freedom and playful abandon, yet with smoothness and careful finish of detail, with extreme lightness and flute-like delicacy in the opening theme, and only a relative degree of power in the climaxes.   Any suggestion of profound or intense emotions, or of genuinely *bravura* style, is out of place.

Minuet from Sonata Op. 7, Grieg.

In speaking of the Minuet, one cannot ignore the remarkably unique and original movement bearing that name in Grieg's Sonata in E minor.   It is typically Norse in character; wild, grotesque, yet weirdly fascinating.   It is a Minuet in form and rhythm, but not in spirit, in the ordinary sense.

The first theme, in heavy chords and octaves, is sombre, fantastic, and ponderous, like a midnight dance of the earth giants, who, according to Norse mythology, inhabited the darksome caves and gorges of the mountains, a rude, malevolent race that waged perpetual war against the Gods.

The Trio is one of Grieg's masterpieces in the line of simple, tenderly appealing, yet, in a way, uncanny melodies, like the sweet, plaintive voice of one of the forest fairies, or "little people," as they were called, who were ever striving to protect humanity, and especially children, from the brutal power of the giants and the vindictive machinations of the small but vicious trolls.

Minuet by W. H. Sherwood.

Those who enjoy a bit of brilliant, wholesome humor and genuine rollicking fun in music will find a treasure in this extremely clever and effective Minuet by Sherwood, the theme of which is taken from the century-old, popular English song known as "Buy a broom."

I would also call attention to two fine, thoroughly musical Minuets, in modern style, by Edgar Sherwood, which, like most good American compositions, deserve to be far better known, and more used than they are.

When will our musical public learn that a foreign origin is not the only criterion of merit!

Other Dance Forms.

In my treatment of Dance Forms in this volume I have not spoken of the Mazurka, although many excellent compositions have been and still are written in this form; partly because I have given the main facts about it in my analysis of Godard's *Second Mazurka* on page 105, partly because no author could write of the Mazurka with the same authority and eloquence as Liszt in his familiar little book on Chopin.

I have also given no attention to the Polka, because although at times a very popular dance, it has never evolved, like the waltz, into a legitimate musical art form, the best example in that line being Raff's Polka de la Reine. The same is true of the Galop.

In regard to the Sarabande, Courante, Gigue, etc., once subdivisions of the Suite, they are now practically obsolete, both as dances and forms of musical composition.

Composers' Index

Composers' Index 231

Alphabetical Index

Alphabetical Index 235

236 Alphabetical Index

DATE DUE